I0818978

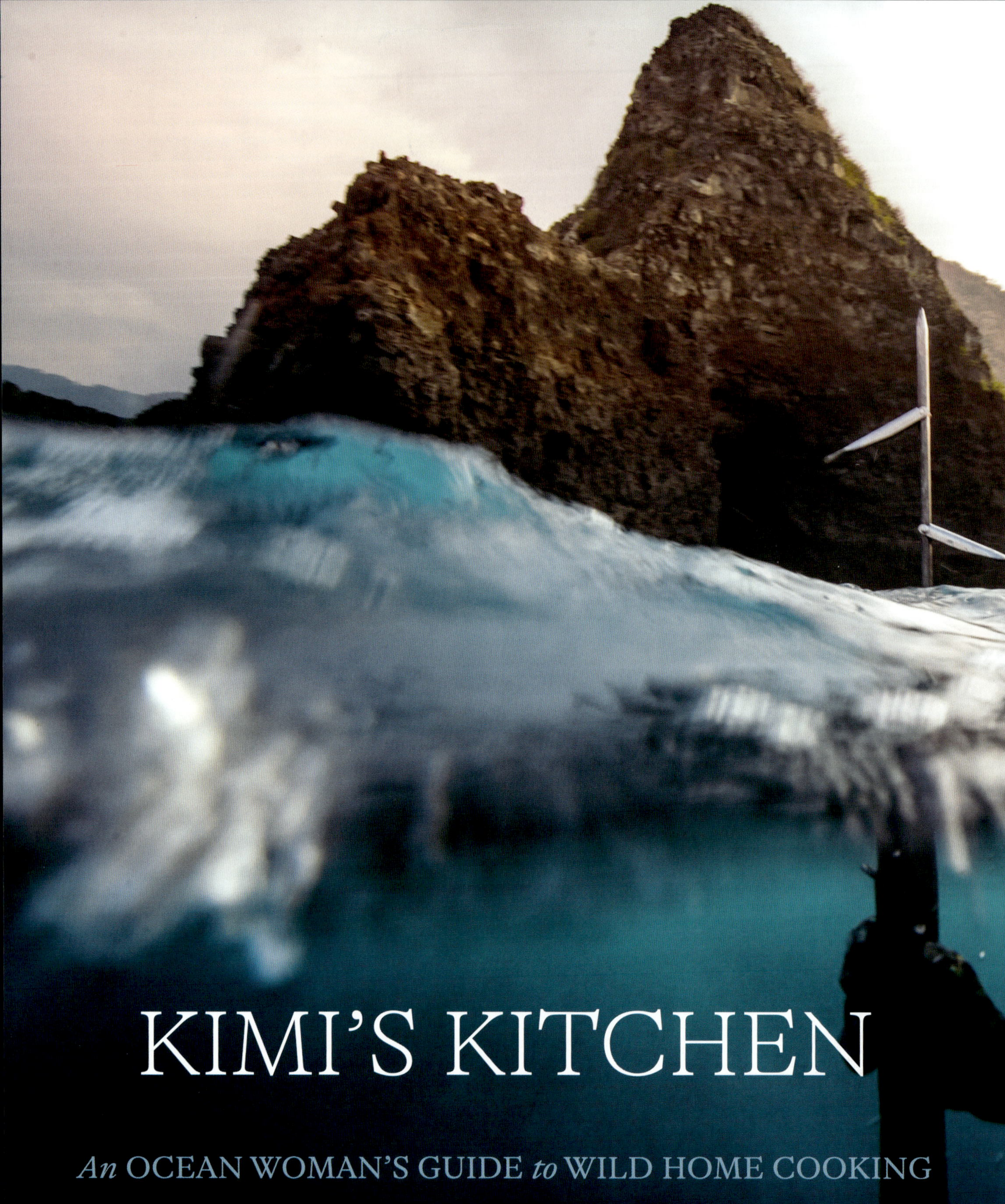

KIMI'S KITCHEN

An OCEAN WOMAN'S GUIDE *to* WILD HOME COOKING

Kimi Werner, Nicole Gormley
& Jennifer Fiedler

"From the moment I met Kimi Werner, I felt that deep, quiet strength—the kind born of the ocean, the ʻāina, and the wisdom of our kūpuna. Kimi is a world-class freediver, a skilled huntress, a true artist with food, and a guardian of the earth. She lives what she teaches. Every dive and every dish are rooted in respect for culture, community, and the next generation. This book is her invitation back to simplicity and balance, to living in rhythm with the natural world. I'm proud to call Kimi my friend, my sister, my teacher. May these pages inspire you to move with reverence, live with purpose, and protect what you love."

—Jason Momoa, actor, filmmaker, entrepreneur, and ocean advocate

"What I admire most about Kimi is her honesty. She's never been afraid to tell me what she really thinks, and that kind of truth is rare and necessary. Years ago, at a Patagonia store opening in Hawaiʻi, someone mentioned wanting to serve little fried fish but couldn't find a fisherman. I heard a voice say, "I know how to catch them. How many do you need?" The next day Kimi returned with a cooler full of little red fish and cleaned them by hand right in our parking lot. That's who she is—generous, grounded, and ready for adventure. Over the years, we have bonded over a shared mission to change the world through the food we eat. I watch every episode of her YouTube channel (sometimes twice) because her food tells a story. This book brings it all together—her values, her underwater adventures, her roots. It's not just a cookbook. It's a reminder of how to live in better balance with the world around us."

—Yvon Chouinard, founder of Patagonia, environmentalist, and author of *Let My People Go Surfing*

"Kimi is one of my favorite people in the world and one of my favorite cooks. Her food is deliberate and passionate. She cooks as a way of honoring her ingredients and honoring her guests. The best thing that could happen for you is getting invited to Kimi's for dinner. The next best thing is to cook from this book."

—Steven Rinella, author and host of *The MeatEater Podcast*

"It's hard not to admire and love Kimi Werner for her incredible career as a spearfisher, but that's just the surface of who she is. She is also one of the nicest people I know and one hell of a cook! From bounties of the sea to hunting and gardening, Kimi shines when cooking for her family and friends. This book captures why we cook, why we gather, and why food matters."

—Brad Leone, chef, author, and food personality

"Like some of the great stoics of our past, Kimi has never shied away from challenging herself to keep it real. For most of us, if the world goes to hell in a handbasket, we would simply not know what to do. Not so with Kimi. She would live just like she's been living: full hearted, in technicolor, and truly off the land and sea. Kimi is the maternal force everybody wants around. She provides, cares, and protects like the true warrior that she is. There is so much humility and power in this book. I don't want to categorize it as any certain thing other than necessary. Read well, soak it up like a needed nutrient, and fall into what true, full-bodied health is."

—Josh Brolin, actor and author of *From Under the Truck*

"Kimi Werner is a badass mana wahine. Whenever she's at the BBQ, the food always tastes better! I'm stoked on this book because I'll cook whatever she tells me."

—Jack Johnson, musician and environmentalist

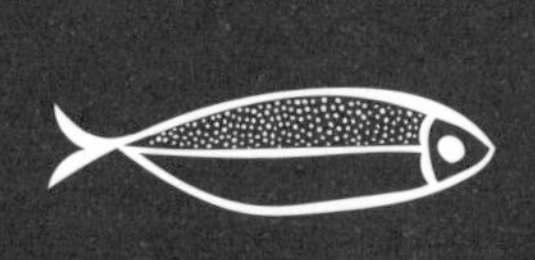

Photography by Nicole Gormley,
Justin Turkowski & Perrin James

TEN SPEED PRESS
California | New York

Dear Buddy,

These pages hold more than recipes. They are the stories of where I came from and where you came from. And long after I'm gone, these recipes will be here to remind you that you will always belong. No matter where you are, you belong to Hawaiʻi, to this earth, to the ocean, and to nature itself. I hope these recipes remind you to be resourceful and scrappy. To use what you have and make it shine. I hope they remind you to stay curious and taste new flavors and never stop seeking and learning from the world around you. I hope they teach you to embrace the struggle and make the best of it because creativity rarely comes from having a wealth of options—it's usually quite the opposite. As long as you have nature, you are not alone. It's who you are and what you're made of and I'm there too. I'm in the trees and rocks and rain and fish and in the ridiculously tiny tomatoes that sprout up from the cracks in the concrete. I'm in these recipes and so are you. So, cook them and eat them and make them your own, my boy. And with every bite, remember who you are and that you are always home.

Contents

My dad's dive crew. Haiku, Maui (1985)

Introduction

My family was quite poor until I was about seven years old, but I remember this time only as magical. I didn't realize that my parents struggled to make ends meet and that the main reason my dad went spearfishing for food was to save money. Nor did I realize that the lessons and values my mom taught me—of respecting nature and using every morsel without waste—was led by her need to be financially resourceful. All I knew is that I was happy living in our rented shack of rotting wood in the rainy and rural town of Haiku, Maui. And that I loved following Dad around in the deep blue sea and watching in awe as he'd hold his breath, disappear into the depths below, and return to the surface with my favorite dinners in hand. Fried fish, sashimi, lobsters, Kona crab—these are the meals that still make me smile when I think back to those times.

I was his cheerleader, always clapping for him at the surface, giddy with delight over his catches. I never actually caught anything myself—I was too young. But I was a devoted tagalong and enjoyed every second in the ocean with him, sometimes so much that I would get distracted by the magic of it all, only to look up and realize that I had no idea where my dad was. The fear was jolting. The ocean immediately seemed bigger and darker, and I suddenly felt so small. But as long as I could look at the very edge of my visibility, I could find the bubbles left by Dad's fins. They would calm me down and assure me that he was near; like finding a trusty street sign while lost, they'd read, "Swim that way!"

My sister and I played in the river behind our house, where we caught crawdads to eat and picked fruit to bring home. We spent many afternoons helping my parents process the fresh fish my dad caught or the animals that my parents raised to feed us.

When I turned seven, things changed dramatically. My parents started making money. They saved up enough to enroll Mom at Maui Community College to get her nursing degree, and my dad's construction business took off. And just like that, our family was thrust into a more civilized way of living. We moved to a subdivision with paved roads and other houses all around us; our days of living in the boonies came to an abrupt end.

Although I grew up in a civilized, "normal" way from there on out, those ocean memories never stopped speaking to me. And neither did my love for food. After high school, I moved to Oʻahu to pursue a degree in culinary arts. I got a job at an Americanized Mexican restaurant as a linc cook, but I hated it. I had no connection to the ingredients or meals I was preparing. I found no creative joy in pumping out the same dishes every night using ingredients all imported from afar. Weighing me down the most was the feeling that I had arrived and no longer had a path unfolding in front of me. I got the degree, got the job, and was starting to fear that this would be it for the rest of my life.

It started to become apparent that those memories of foraging meals from the ocean were the most treasured moments of my entire upbringing. At the time, I thought that lifestyle was a way of the past that no longer existed in this modern world. That is, until one day after competing in a paddling regatta, I watched as a few guys in my canoe club gathered around a small barbecue. The fish they placed over the fire were ones that I recognized from my youth. Kole, menpachi, and goatfish. When I asked where they got these fish, they simply said, "We went diving." Seeing this memory come to life in this present-day world felt like gold to me. I begged those guys to take me along and told them that I loved to dive. But the more I talked, the more I must've sounded like a liability—claiming to love spearfishing while explaining that my experience consisted of tagging along with my dad when I was five years old. Needless to say, they didn't call.

But the spark had been ignited, and my yearning for relearning freediving grew so strong that I finally decided I'd just go on my own. At the age of twenty-four, I drove out to the North Shore with a newly purchased three-prong spear and fins. When I got out of the car and started walking to the beach, I felt disabled with intimidation and anxiety. I felt like everyone was looking at me—this girl with a spear—and that everyone knew I had no idea what I was doing. I tried to hide my spear as I walked past beachgoers and slipped into the water.

The ocean was choppy, making the water hazy, and the more I tried to push my anxiety away, the more frantic I felt. I was scared and uncomfortable and felt like this whole thing was a stupid idea. But right when I was going to finally obey my demanding urge to turn around and return to shore, a small wind swell in the distance broke on the surface.

And when it did, I saw bubbles.

My body was triggered into a state of calm. The same comfort of relief swept over me just as it had when I was four years old, when Dad's bubbles said, "Swim this way!" My muscle memory took over and I leaned into it. Eventually, I ended up swimming over a small reef in about twenty-five feet of water. I held my breath and kicked down. The reef was loaded with those same fish of my childhood. Over and over again, I let my spear fly at them. I missed a lot. It was hard. They were fast little suckers, but the hunt was on! Hours flew by in the ocean and by the end of the day, I returned to shore with five fish on my stringer.

The woman who got out of the water that day was not the same woman who had entered it. I held my spear straight with my head high as I walked on the beach back to my car. I kept staring at my catch and felt the most primal sense of satisfaction I had ever felt. I was a lioness, returning from my hunt with food to bring home. And that night, when I simply cleaned, scored, and seasoned these fish with salt and pepper, then fried them, I felt like I had made the most delicious meal of my culinary career.

This day changed my life. It felt like falling in love. Nothing else in life really seemed to matter—I just wanted more of this happiness. I dreamed about fish in my sleep. I saw them every time I closed my eyes.

Eventually, the same canoe paddling boys who once avoided my persistence started calling when I started showing up at barbecues with my own catch to contribute. Soon, I got the dive partners of my dreams when I was introduced to Kalei Fernandez, Wayde Hayashi, and Andy Tamasese.

Culinary school was my path, but I found my purpose in the sea.

These guys were the best divers in Hawai'i, and once they took me under their wings, my diving went to the next level. I had no idea I could dive a hundred feet and deeper until they taught me how. The possibilities became endless, and within a few years, I found myself the United States Spearfishing National Champion.

This got me recognition among the spearfishing community, and soon I was getting offers to travel for my diving. I kept competing until I realized it was taking away from the joy I felt in the ocean. Winning became all I thought about. I'd swim out to get food but think only about how many points each fish would be worth. I didn't like what it was doing to me. My roots were all about the ocean giving me food, not trophies, and I found a deeper sense of self and passion when I was cooking for my friends and family and tinkering with recipes—frying, grilling, and seasoning the hard-won sustenance—than when I was just winning. So I stepped away from competing and, to my surprise, that didn't hinder any of the opportunities.

My freediving has taken me to depths below 150 feet and to every continent. I've been able to spear dogtooth tuna in Africa, cod in the Arctic Circle, giant yellowtail in Chile, and so many other delicious fish of the world. I've swum with orcas in Norway, great white sharks in Mexico, sperm whales in the Caribbean, and leopard seals in the icy waters of Antarctica. It's given me a community of ocean-loving friends across the world, partnerships with a spectrum of great brands, and the ability to do what I love for a living. But it's never felt as full circle as it does right now, living in a simple home near the ocean with a humble but prosperous garden and going to the sea with my husband and my three-prong spear to fetch food for our son, Buddy.

From the roots of where I came from to the winds of where I've been, there's so much of the life and lessons I've learned woven into the recipes in this book. Knowing where to find food and how to cook it is a combination that will give you far more than just survival. It can give you community and an inner sense of belonging no matter where you go. As you flip through these pages and learn of my journey, I hope that maybe it evokes a curiosity in you. I hope that maybe you look at the edible plants growing in your own backyard, or learn about the fish that surround your own coastlines, or explore any invasive species in your ecosystem that might just happen to be tasty. Or maybe you just get to know your neighbors and their fruit trees, your local butcher or artisan fisherman, or check out your farmers' market more often. I hope that this book inspires you to look a little closer at your own local ecosystem and community and connect with them through cooking and eating. Perhaps by making our home cooking just a little more wild, we can join hands and tighten the gap that often forms between us and nature.

The Rules

Keep your knives sharp.

You don't have to be religious to gather and give thanks for food.

Respect the plants and animals that feed us.

A fresh ingredient in its prime, ready to be prepared with love, is always and absolutely a good reason to cancel plans and change your schedule.

Leftovers are absolute gold. Do not neglect them; transform them!

High heat is my jam. It keeps me present and on my toes. It browns. It sears. It's the flavor and texture maker. But if a fast pace causes anxiety, do not be too stubborn to turn it down.

Learn to appreciate the off-cuts. Using the whole animal will give you resourcefulness, creativity, deliciousness, and health.

Pick fresh flowers for your kitchen as often as possible.

If you don't have a certain ingredient, ask yourself if something else can stand in its place. Activate innovation.

Fresh citrus is as essential as salt in my house.

Know how to make a fire.

Eat the bait!

Before you harvest an animal ask yourself: Is it my appetite or my ego buzzing?

Get to know your local ecosystems and realize which species are becoming scarcer, and act accordingly.

Return all fish guts and scales to the ocean or the soil.

Listen to elders and learn about the ways they eat. If you can provide those meals to them, do it. Keep it going.

Let your kids get involved. Let them slow you down. Don't stress the mess.

My Pantry

These are ingredients that I reach for constantly. Together, they make up the flavor profile of my cooking.

Oils and Fats

Frying Oil: I use olive oil for just about everything, including pan-frying a meal for my family. But if I need a lot of oil because I'm making multiple batches of deep-fried octopus or serving enough fried fish for a party, I'll tend to go with an oil that withstands higher heat for long periods of time. Avocado oil is great for this.

Olive Oil: From dressing and dipping to sautéing and even frying, I find olive oil to be much more versatile than it's usually given credit for. Using the good stuff is important to me. I love Kirkland Signature 100% Spanish Extra Virgin Olive Oil for the price if you use it as generously as I do.

Salted Butter: I don't believe in unsalted butter. My favorite butter is Kirkland Signature Grass-Fed Butter from New Zealand. I cook with it often and cut it thick like cheese if I'm eating it on a piece of good bread.

Seasonings

Chili Pepper Water (page 34): Chili peppa watah (the correct way to say it) is a main staple here in Hawai'i. I tend to make mine on the salty, spicy, tangy side because I want a single splash of it to add some immediate punch and brightness to a meal that needs it.

Crunchy Garlic Chili Oil (page 191): I love making my own version of chili crisp because I prefer avocado oil as the base instead of the typical canola oil base of those sold in stores. This is the most addicting thing. Make it, keep it in your fridge, and thank me later.

Fish Sauce: This can be aggressively pungent stuff, taking over your whole kitchen with its fishy smell as soon as a drop of it hits a hot pan. But, wow, does it give dishes the savory satisfaction of umami in an instant. I like experimenting with different brands from Asian grocery stores.

Flaky Sea Salt: Always have lots of flaky, good-quality salt on hand. I have a huge tub of Maldon salt that never leaves my countertop, as well as at least two more of the same size in my pantry for backup at all times. I tend to use this salt a bit too freely and need to remind myself to switch to finer-grain table salt for things like soup and sauces that will dissolve that beautiful flake anyway. It's still hard for me. I like to live indulgently.

Fresh Garlic: I know it takes time to peel and chop the cloves, but it's always worth it and the result is far superior to the already minced jarred garlic.

Fresh Ginger: This is something I buy at least every other week. I love to keep my ginger fresh, as it's juicier and easier to peel than when it gets old and starts to shrivel. Fresh ginger should be easy to snap and easy to peel with a spoon.

Freshly Ground Black Pepper: There's no need for any other kind. My pepper mill is by Männkitchen, and I always have it set to a very coarse grind.

Hawaiian Sea Salt: I use coarse Hawaiian sea salt for massaging octopus to tenderize and clean it; a nice coarse salt helps get that scrubbing going while seasoning it at the same time. If you can't find Hawaiian sea salt, coarse kosher salt is a great substitute.

Shoyu: This is the word for "soy sauce" in Japanese, and that's what we call it here in Hawai'i. When I started doing YouTube cooking videos, I once referred to it as soy sauce, and my sister called, immediately exclaiming, "Who are you?" I will refer to it as shoyu from now on. My favorite brand is Yamasa.

Toasted Sesame Oil: This oil has such a beautiful aroma and nutty flavor. It's the only oil I know to have its own sense of umami already in it, and it's a glorious thing.

Miscellaneous

Bouillon: I love the brand Better Than Bouillon. Up until this brand came along the only options for store-bought stock were bouillon cubes or cartons of bland broth. Game changer!

Coconut Milk: Nothing will ever beat coconut milk freshly pressed from mature, sweet, grated coconut meat, but I live in Hawai'i and I rarely squeeze my own, so I don't expect you to, either. Chaokoh is the brand of canned coconut milk that I have on hand, but any canned coconut milk brand that is unsweetened and full-fat should do the job. Hawaiian Sun Frozen Coconut Milk is even better.

Maple Syrup: Please, use the real stuff only. I won't even look at the artificial syrup we used to put on pancakes as kids. My husband is from Minnesota, so we always have a variety of small-batch good stuff that my mother-in-law sends consistently, but there are so many great brands in stores. Just make sure the label says "pure maple syrup."

Mayonnaise: I grew up on Best Foods mayo and I still love it. Its flavor and consistency are amazing and work so well for any recipe that calls for mayonnaise. But in my effort to choose healthier oils, I have strayed and tried Primal Kitchen mayo made with avocado oil, and I must say, I love it. Its consistency is great, it has no weird flavors, and it's extra lemony, which to me is always a good thing. So, I find myself switching off between buying those two brands, depending on what's available and how much I feel like spending.

Rice: In Hawai'i, we use white Calrose rice, either short or medium grain. It's not jasmine rice and it's not fall-off-your-fork rice. It's slightly wet and sticky when cooked and can hold a shape when pressed.

My Equipment

I believe that hands are often our best tools. But here are some other ones that make cooking easier and the food more delicious.

Blender: It's not just for smoothies. It's the secret to my hollandaise sauce, it makes my bisque extra silky, and it's a great hack for making poi at home.

Cast-Iron Skillets: They are heavy but special. Learn to love them and know that the more you use them, the better they behave.

Chest Freezer: A freezer is a beautiful thing and a great way to stock up on abundance to save for later. But it's a total sin to use it as a black hole to send good ingredients to a forgotten graveyard of freezer burn. Never do that. I think a standing freezer would probably be a great idea, but I have a chest freezer where I can see only the very top layer of what's in it and everything else gets buried. It's very important to me to take inventory often. I dig through it a lot and try to put the oldest items or the poorly packaged ones

on top so that they get used first. My freezer is filled with wild game, fish, steamed breadfruit, cubed taro, and cooked spinach. Whatever is in yours, you should know about it because that's the only way it's going to make it to a dinner plate.

Cooking Chopsticks: My mom always cooked with cooking chopsticks (which are extra-long), and I have taken after her. They provide more space between your hands and heat for safety but offer the same dexterity and intuitive flow of stirring, flipping, and pushing food. If you don't know how to use chopsticks, it's not too late to learn!

Electric Pressure Cooker: I love my speedy little Instant Pot that makes tough meats tender and cuts the time of lengthy braising and steaming into mere minutes. My sister bought me one years ago even though I didn't think I needed one. I get it now, Christy, I get it.

Electric Smoker and Grill: I never thought I'd want a grill that can be plugged in. I always loved cooking over wood or hot coals, and when Traeger offered to send me an electric wood pellet–burning smoker and grill, I thought I'd be sure to hate it. Man, was I wrong. It's almost annoying how easy it is to perfectly cook everything from huge roasts of wild game to delicately smoked fish. There are many smoked recipes in here and that's all Traeger's fault. They made it too easy for me to achieve smoky flavor and preserve fresh catches for weeks to come.

Good Set of Knives and Honer: This is another area where my collection has grown to the point where I had to cut myself off. But, all you really need is a good chef's knife—you can achieve anything with that alone. But if I had to choose just four knives to own, it would be in this order: Chef's knife, fillet knife, sashimi knife, and bread knife. I always keep a honer in my knife drawer and use it often. It can quickly bring back a sharp edge to a blade with a few swipes.

Mortar and Pestle: It seems like other cultures know that cutting doesn't release the same flavors and oils that smashing and crushing can, yet most of us continue to only chop away. It's ingrained in me too, and I need to remind myself to get out my mortar and pestle. When I do, it's worth it.

Vacuum Sealer: This is an important tool for keeping frozen food in top quality.

Wooden Cutting Boards: Wooden cutting boards over plastic, always. I love beautiful boards and own too many of them, but I adore my collection. And they're not just for cutting! They are also for serving, so I love having a variety of organic shapes and different sizes. When slicing roasted meats, I always have a couple options with a drip groove to catch all the juices.

Wooden Spoons: Own a wooden spoon that feels good in your hands and makes your soul happy.

My Garden

- Flat-leaf Parsley
- Green Onions
- Thai Basil
- Chives
- Mint
- Oregano
- Rosemary
- Collard Greens
- Spinach
- Kale
- Hawaiian Chiles
- Papayas
- Limes

Sourcing Fish

As fishing and farming become more industrialized on a mass scale, our oceans and natural world are paying the price. My brother Randy Kosaki is one of the world's top fish conservation biologists and served as the National Oceanic and Atmospheric Administration's deputy superintendent of the Papahānaumokuākea Marine National Sanctuary (one of the largest conservation areas on Earth). In other words, he's the biggest fish nerd I know. He's also a fisherman who feels strongly that globally, we need to be fishing in a way that's sustainable not just now but generations into the future. Randy inspires me to believe that, by changing our practices, it's entirely possible that we could get quite a bit more protein out of the ocean than we are now without overfishing.

So much about cooking delicious, sustainable meals from the sea comes down to knowing how your seafood was sourced and harvested. I know this can be really hard to gauge when shopping for fish, as information can be difficult to find. That's why I really encourage you to try to get to know your local fishers or fishmongers. If you have neighbors, friends, or anyone in your community who fishes or hunts, try to source directly from them. Look for the people with coolers and boats and ask them to point you in the right direction. Local farmers' markets are also a good place to start. Seek out the people closest to the actual harvest and learn directly from them.

You can search online for your local community-supported fishery, or CSF for short. More and more CSFs work to connect customers directly to fishermen and their catches through memberships or weekly subscription boxes. Every place, ecosystem, and fishery is incredibly different, so it's difficult to give broad and general rules where one size fits all, but the answer typically lies in your local community.

To assess the freshness of fish, here are a few recommendations to guide you:

- **Smell the fish.** It should smell fresh like the ocean, not stinky or overly fishy. It's okay for it to smell a bit briny, but it shouldn't smell "off" or like it's spoiling.
- **Feel the fish.** It shouldn't easily give to the touch or be so soft that it's mushy.
- **Avoid wet fish.** It should not be sitting in its own juices or in too much moisture.
- **Look at the fish's eyes.** If you are selecting a whole fish, they should be clear and vibrant, not sunken and milky.
- **Look at the gills.** If the fish still have them, they should be a vibrant red.

Raw Fish

When it comes to eating fish raw, you should follow certain precautions, especially with any fish that have spent any part of their lives living in freshwater. Salmon spend most of their lives at sea, but they still come from freshwater habitats and carry freshwater parasites with them that are easily killed when the meat is cooked or frozen for a few days. You might be surprised to know that even the most beautiful sashimi-grade salmon has been frozen, then defrosted, before being served raw in restaurants. However, when it comes to fresh tuna, which have lived their entire lives in the ocean, I prefer to avoid freezing it if I'm going to eat it raw. Ocean fish don't carry the same parasites, and slow home freezing can deteriorate the quality and color of such a delicate meat like tuna, making it less desirable to eat raw. A good rule of thumb is to eat ocean fish raw within a week of being caught and to make sure that it has been stored and handled correctly (see page 247).

1

A Maui Childhood

Dishes That Raised Me

If I were to describe myself in two parts, I'd say, "I'm half hunter, half hippie." But what I'm really saying is that I'm the product of my mom and dad. My dad, Chris Werner, the hunter, was born in New Mexico but moved to California when he was five. At nineteen, he enlisted in the US Air Force and, after four years of active duty in the Vietnam War, he went to visit his older brother in Maui and never lived anywhere else again. He was taken in by a Hawaiian-Filipino family in the rice camps of Haiku. They taught him to free-dive and spearfish. They used empty plastic Clorox bottles as their buoys with string to hold their fish, and they made their own spearguns by hand, using butter knives for triggers. They'd share their catches with everyone in the rice camp and trade fish to the fish market in Pā'ia for Primo beer.

My dad loved these days on Maui. Things were simple and free. He tells me of the generosity of the Hawaiians who took him in. He boasts that there was only one cop who would patrol the rural countryside of Maui, and he delightfully reminisces about his favorite gas station that would give everyone LSD during the holidays if they filled up their tanks.

And one day at a friend's party, probably fueled up by that gas station, he met a beautiful Japanese hippie named June.

June Michiko Nakaguma was born and raised in Honolulu. Her mom, Margaret, was from Ka'a'awa, O'ahu, and she worked in the pineapple cannery and later became a cook at a restaurant.

To say that my mom had a hard upbringing would be a major understatement. She grew up in a family where children were to be seen but not heard, and she obeyed those rules, quietly suppressing her own needs and emotions even when her father took his own life when she was fourteen. She worked at the pineapple cannery when she was fifteen, handing over every paycheck to help support her mother and four siblings. At seventeen, my grandma kicked her out of the house as punishment for getting pregnant. Mom had the courage and love to give her baby up for adoption at birth in hopes of giving him a better opportunity at life than what she had. (Forty years later, we reunited with this beautiful being who is my fish nerd brother, Randy.)

My dad still smiles when he talks about the night he met my mom. In the weeks that followed, he would drive his motorbike to go on date after date with her. Dad brags about courting Mom through diving. "Once I found out how much she loved lobster—and I mean, she'd suck the guts right out of the head, gross!—I knew how to really impress her."

It was my dad who taught me to dive even if I never touched a spear at the time. He'd put me on his back, hike me down the cliffs of Haiku, and let me drift along with him in the ocean as he fetched dinner to feed our whole family. He introduced me to the beautiful underwater world. He taught me the importance of being able to relax in the water. He showed me firsthand the beauty of catching our own food. He is the absolute foundation of me becoming a spearfisher and hunter. But it was my mom who not only taught me to cook but also drilled

Top: My childhood home—Haiku, Maui.
Bottom: My favorite pink mask.

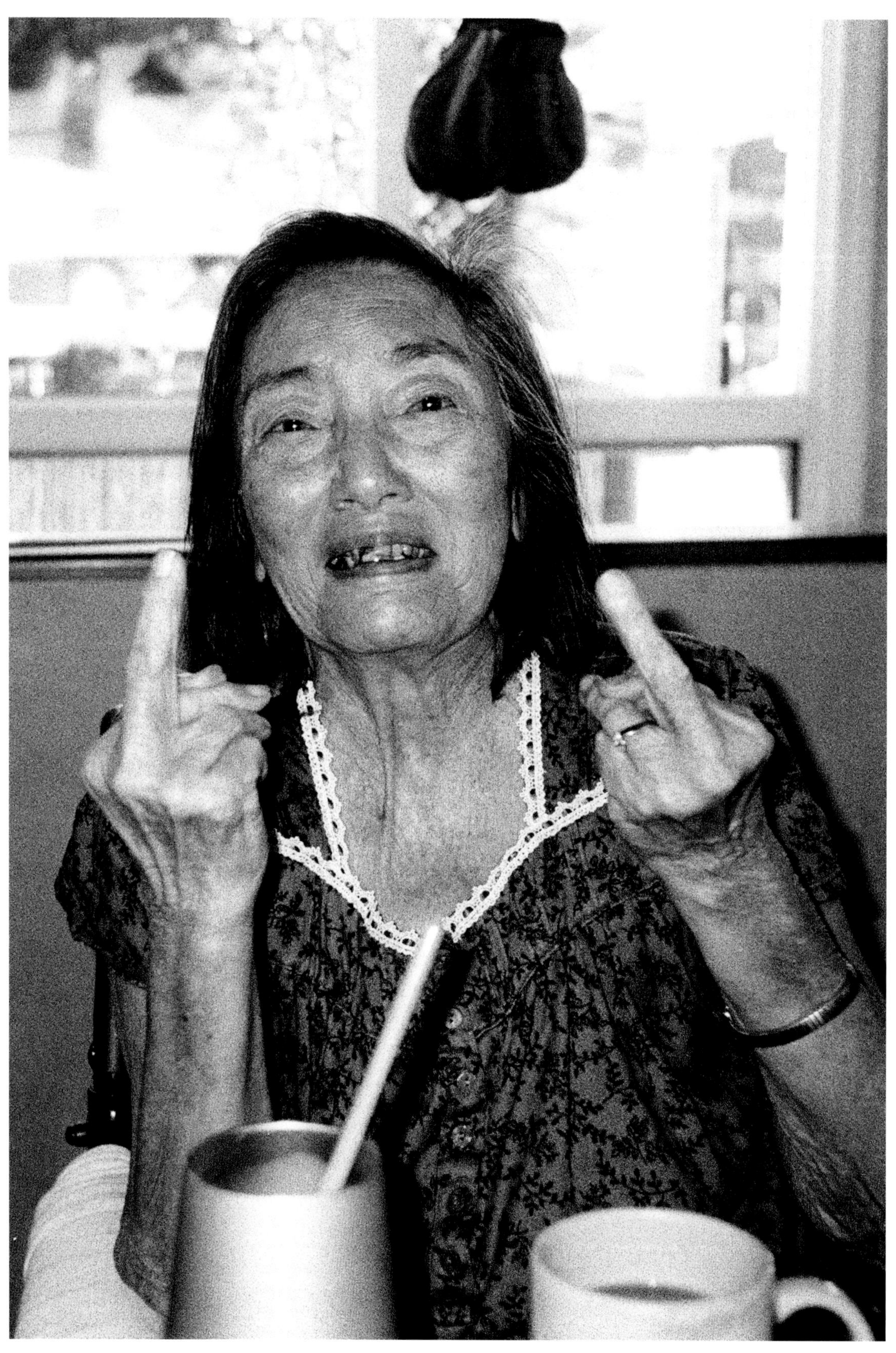

Even now, in her eighties with Alzheimer's, my mom is still an absolute pistol. It's her way of rebelling against her younger years of being taught to be seen but not heard and of breaking that cycle for us.

into all of us—my dad and uncles included—how to respect the natural world and how to give back and take care of that which takes care of us.

Mom taught me how to make a fire when I was eight. To use real butter and not be afraid of fat. She never wasted anything. She'd shoo my dad out of the way when he would try to fillet a fish because he'd leave too much meat on the bones. She taught us to never take more than we needed and use everything we had. Back then, it wasn't called sustainability but rather common sense that when something takes care of you, you treat it right and make sure it lasts. And boy, could she cook.

Food was how she shared love, and she had so much of it to share. "Hungry, Baby?" she'd always ask. It was practically her way of saying "hello." Just imagining the sound of her soothing voice asking those two caring words makes my heart ache with warmth, love, and nostalgia.

When I look at the recipes in this chapter, I see my parents' resourcefulness in using what we had and my mom's love for taking care of people. I see that it wasn't just us as a family that she fed. She cooked in batches so that we had leftovers, and she was always ready to cook or heat something up for anyone who would drop by. Nothing fancy, just really savory, hearty comfort food full of flavor and full of love. People have always gravitated toward her because of her ninja skills in real talk. She stood up for what she felt was right and encouraged us to speak our minds. She is so embedded in me. I have a deep need to feed people, and like her I love through food. These recipes have my own personal spin. I often substitute wild game for the store-bought meat we ate as kids, but this food sums up the backbone of my family cooking.

Ugly Dumplings

(A Fish-Filled Tribute to My Mom's Gau Gee)

Makes about 70 dumplings

No one makes gau gee like my mom makes gau gee. I remember this dish, which is similar to a fried wonton or gyoza, always being requested for potlucks and holiday gatherings. Mom's gau gee were Chinese-influenced with ground pork, shrimp, and water chestnuts. They took a lot of work and were always made on the day of the event or gathering. She would stuff and fold enough gau gee to feed a small village, all by hand, and she always let us help, even though my gau gee were messy and bursting at the seams. She took her time and fried batch after batch in her cast-iron skillet. The hardest part was trying to wait for the gau gee to cool down enough to try the first one. The second hardest part of the whole process was restraining ourselves to not eat all of Mom's hard work before going to the potluck or party.

My dumplings are not my mom's crispy gau gee, but rather a similar labor of love that honors it. They satisfy my craving for Mom's savory snacks, but I feel better about devouring these bundles of veggies and fish than I do the same amount of deep-fried pork pockets. I tend to use circular gyoza wrappers, but any wonton-style wrappers will work. My ugly dumplings can be made with just about any fish out there—it doesn't have to be the most prized or sashimi-grade fish. It can be a previously frozen or a lesser-favored fish, as all the ginger, veggies, and herbs do a lot to balance and enhance the flavor.

I mince the fish by hand rather than use a food processor because I want every bite to be meaty, not mushy. I love to put a lot of veggies in my filling and serve the dumplings with a spicy, tangy vinegar shoyu sauce. My dumpling folding has not improved all that much since childhood, hence the name of this recipe. But I've found that even the ugliest dumplings are still delicious. You can fry, steam, or boil them, but my favorite preparation is browning them in a little bit of olive oil, then steaming to finish. These can be stuffed and folded ahead of time and frozen to cook later. Just don't let them get smashed or stuck together when freezing! When you're ready to eat, continue the recipe from the step that starts with "To cook the dumpings." They will defrost in the pan. Add 2 minutes to the covered cooking time.

Note: *If you end up with extra fish filling, make patties and sauté them.*

continued

Ugly Dumplings

continued

Dumplings

¼ cup toasted sesame oil

1 large carrot, peeled and minced (about ¾ cup)

1 head bok choy, stems minced and leaves finely chopped

2 large ribs celery, minced (about ¾ cup)

½ yellow onion, minced (about ¾ cup)

4 garlic cloves, minced

3 tablespoons minced ginger

2 pounds boneless, skinless fish (any fish will work, from scraps to prime cuts)

¾ cup sliced green onions, white and green parts

One 8-ounce can water chestnuts, drained and minced

½ cup finely chopped fresh cilantro

3 eggs

2 teaspoons flaky sea salt

1 teaspoon freshly ground black pepper

70 dumpling wrappers (I prefer gyoza or mandu)

Olive oil for sautéing

Dipping Sauce

½ cup shoyu

⅓ cup white vinegar

2 tablespoons sliced green onions, white and green parts

1 tablespoon toasted sesame oil

Freshly ground black pepper

1 tablespoon Crunchy Garlic Chili Oil (page 191) or chili crisp (optional)

White sesame seeds for garnishing (optional)

To make the dumpling filling: In a medium skillet over medium-high heat, warm the sesame oil. Add the carrot, bok choy stems, celery, and onion, and stir occasionally. Once the veggies start to sweat and soften, 3 to 5 minutes, add the bok choy leaves, garlic, and ginger. Cook until soft, 1 more minute, and set the sautéed veggies aside to cool.

Using a sharp knife, mince the fish and put it in a large mixing bowl. Add the green onions, water chestnuts, cilantro, eggs, sautéed veggies, salt, and pepper to the bowl. Mix everything together until thoroughly and evenly combined.

To wrap the dumplings: Set up a dumpling wrapping station by laying out the following items, all within arms' reach: a small bowl of water, the dumpling wrappers, a tablespoon, the dumpling filling, and a baking sheet or large plate. Assemble the dumplings by dipping your finger in the water, then run it along one half of the outside perimeter of a wrapper to wet it. Scoop 1 tablespoon of the filling in the center of the dumpling wrapper, then fold one side of the wrapper over the filling to meet the opposite side. Press lightly to seal the edge. If you're feeling fancy, pinch the wrapper together to form crimped pleats, but it's not necessary. Place the finished dumplings on the baking sheet or plate and repeat with the rest of the wrappers and filling.

To cook the dumplings: In a large skillet over medium-high heat, add enough olive oil to coat the skillet, and warm the oil. Working in batches, place ten to twelve dumplings in the skillet, giving them enough space so they don't touch. Cook until the dumplings begin to brown, 2 to 3 minutes, then add ½ cup of water to the skillet. Cover and cook for 3 minutes longer, then uncover and use a spatula to transfer the dumplings onto a platter. Repeat with the remaining dumplings.

To make the dipping sauce: In a small bowl, combine the shoyu, white vinegar, green onions, sesame oil, and black pepper. Stir in the crunchy garlic chili oil and sesame seeds, if using, and serve alongside the hot dumplings.

Smoky Spinach Dip and Crispy ʻUlu Chips

Serves 4 to 6 as an appetizer

Spinach Dip

5 ounces Cured and Smoked Venison (page 97) or cooked bacon, finely chopped

10 ounces frozen, chopped spinach, defrosted and squeezed dry

One 8-ounce can water chestnuts, drained and finely chopped

1 cup mayonnaise

1 cup sour cream

4 ounces cream cheese, at room temperature

¼ cup finely chopped green onions, white and green parts

2 tablespoons dried dill

Crispy ʻUlu Chips

Neutral oil or beef tallow for frying (see Note)

½ medium firm green ʻulu (breadfruit; about 1 pound), steamed (see page 122) and sliced thinly

Flaky sea salt

Note: *The oil can be almost anything you would use for frying, such as avocado or olive, but if you happen to have any delicious beef tallow or rendered fat, now is the time to use it because it adds a delicious flavor.*

Mom's spinach dip was always a top request when we would go to potluck gatherings. I know spinach dip is a common casual snack, but Mom's was special. And that's because her recipe had water chestnuts and this super-salty dried beef. It was dried beef sliced into paper-thin circles that came in a jar and was kept unrefrigerated on store shelves, so it was really, really salty. When I made this recipe as a young adult, I had a hard time finding the same dried beef in stores; it was so old-school. In fact, aside from Mom's spinach dip, I have no idea what it was used for. But recently, when Justin's spinach was taking over our entire backyard, I remembered Mom's dip and recreated it with our homegrown spinach and smoked, cured venison and served it with freshly fried ʻulu (breadfruit) chips. Wow, was it a winning combo on this nostalgic classic.

To make the spinach dip: In a medium bowl, add the venison, spinach, water chestnuts, mayonnaise, sour cream, cream cheese, green onions, and dill. Stir to thoroughly combine.

Chill the dip for at least 3 hours or up to overnight before serving.

To make the ʻulu chips: Place a wire rack over a baking pan and set it near the stove. In a large skillet over high heat, heat ½ inch of oil. Once the oil is hot and shimmering, about 2 minutes, work in batches and gently place the sliced ʻulu in the skillet in a single layer with no overlap. When the bottom of the ʻulu has browned, 2 to 3 minutes, flip the pieces over. When they are evenly golden brown on both sides, about 5 minutes total, transfer the pieces to the prepared wire rack to cool. Repeat with the remaining ʻulu. Season with salt.

Fried Fish Bones and Chili Pepper Water

Serves 6 to 8 as an appetizer

Frame of one 5- to 7-pound fish, such as aku (skipjack tuna), or several frames of smaller fish, fillets removed and head discarded

Flaky sea salt and freshly ground black pepper

Olive oil for frying

3 garlic cloves, smashed

Chili Pepper Water (recipe follows) for garnishing

I loved helping my grandma scale and clean the fish that my dad would bring home. She wouldn't waste anything: She would put the guts and blood in her always thriving garden, cut the meat into sashimi and poke, and then fry up the bones for dinner. Fried fish bones—especially from aku—is a classic, old-school Hawai'i-style dish that we'd see at gatherings, with chili pepper water on the side. When I'm filleting fish and know that I'll be frying up the bones, I'll purposely leave more meat on them. (You don't eat the actual bones but rather pick off the meat like mini fish ribs.)

With a cleaver or sharp knife, chop the fish frame into 3- to 4-inch pieces. Generously season the pieces with salt and pepper.

Line a platter with paper towels, or set a wire rack over a baking pan and set near the stove. In a large cast-iron pan or heavy skillet over medium-high heat, warm ¼ inch of olive oil until it sizzles when a piece of fish is dipped in, about 3 minutes. Working in batches, add the fish pieces and garlic to the pan and cook until the garlic has browned, 2 to 3 minutes. Transfer the garlic to the prepared platter or wire rack. Continue cooking the fish until browned, 4 to 5 minutes in total. Flip and cook the fish on the other side until browned and crispy, 2 to 3 minutes, then transfer to the prepared platter or wire rack to cool. Repeat the process with the remaining fish pieces. Garnish with the fried garlic and chili pepper water and serve immediately.

Fish Alternatives

Yellowtail
Salmon
Cod

Chili Pepper Water

Makes ½ cup

2 habanero chiles or 8 Hawaiian chiles, chopped

2 garlic cloves, chopped

1 teaspoon coarse salt

3 tablespoons white vinegar

¼ cup water

This chili pepper water recipe is quick and easy and makes enough for one meal. I'm super flexible on the spice level, but I prefer mine salty because I like to use it as a seasoning. If you happen to have extra, the chili pepper water will last covered in the fridge for a long time—maybe forever?

Use a mortar and pestle to grind the chiles, garlic, and salt to a chunky paste. (Alternatively, use a knife to finely chop.) Add the vinegar and water and stir to combine. Pour the mixture into a glass bottle or jar. Serve immediately or store, covered, in the fridge.

Jang-jorim

(Spicy Shoyu Braised Beef)

Serves 4 to 6

2 pounds boneless venison front shoulder or shanks, or beef chuck, cut into 2-inch cubes

2 cups water

⅓ cup shoyu

4 garlic cloves, chopped

3 green or red jalapeño chiles (or more if you like it extra spicy)

Cooked white rice for serving

My grandma was Japanese, but she cooked all kinds of meals in our house—Hawaiian, Filipino, Chinese, and Korean. She also grew jalapeño chiles like it was nobody's business. Jang-jorim was a family favorite that put those jalapeños to good use. It's salty and spicy and you definitely need some white rice to balance the extremes of those two traits. I can remember how the whole house would smell when she was braising the meat and chiles in a shoyu-based broth. My grandma would always use beef chuck cuts. These days, I have wild game at home, so I make mine with venison. Wild game is much leaner than domestically raised beef, so if you are using the former, whether it's sheep, venison, or elk, opt for the cuts that have a lot of sinew. They get a really bad rep for being tough and chewy as heck, but these are the very best cuts for slow cooking and braising. With two hours of braising, their collagen will slowly break down into this gelatinous goodness that emulates fat and makes each bite of meat so tender, juicy, and soft. It's important to use cuts like the front shoulder, ribs, shanks, or neck that contain such sinew because other cuts, when cooked like this, will be dry in texture.

In a large pot over medium-high heat, add the venison, water, shoyu, garlic, and jalapeños, and stir to combine. Cover the pot, bring to a boil over medium-high heat, then lower the heat to a simmer and cook for 30 minutes. Using a wooden spoon, break open the jalapeños and stir gently to release more of their spiciness. Let simmer until the meat breaks apart easily with a fork, about 90 minutes. Serve over white rice.

Note: *If you're reheating these as leftovers, make sure you add some water to dilute the shoyu-based broth. The jang-jorim will last covered in the fridge for up to 3 days.*

Chinese-Style Steamed Fish with Ginger Sesame Sauce

Serves 2 to 4

1½ pounds whole goatfish, gutted and scaled

Shoyu for drizzling

Ginger Sesame Sauce (recipe follows) for serving

Fish Alternatives

Snapper
Rockfish
Branzino

I'll never forget the first time I tried Chinese-style steamed fish. I had been tagging along with Dad and Uncle Mabu on a dive. Uncle Mabu speared a moana kali, a big, beautiful goatfish with purple and pink hues. Uncle Mabu was so excited to prepare this fish for us. He picked up a few ingredients from the market and we all gathered in a nearby valley in Haiku. My dad and I started making a fire while my uncle began dicing a lot of fresh ginger. He prepared his beautiful fish, wrapped it in foil, and steamed it over the fire. In a small pot on the side, he heated up some peanut oil until it was absolutely smoking. He topped the fish with a bunch of fresh cilantro and made everything sizzle as he poured the smoking oil over it all and finished it with some shoyu. When I took my first bite, every sense of my being screamed in delight: I'd never tasted anything like that before and I wanted more! Although finishing with the traditional sizzling peanut oil is a fun party trick, these days I opt for topping the steamed fish with an olive oil–based ginger sesame sauce because it's less messy and equally delicious. I like to serve this with the Collard Greens with Shoyu and Butter (page 116).

Lay the fish horizontally on a cutting board. Make a series of vertical incisions along the fish body, spacing each cut about 2 inches apart and going deep enough to hit the bone. Cut at an angle to create more surface area to cover with the ginger sesame sauce later. Flip the fish over and repeat on the other side.

Choose a large pot or skillet that can fit the entire fish. If the fish doesn't fit whole in your biggest pot or skillet, cut it in half or in thirds. (Once it has finished steaming, you can arrange it back together to look whole again.)

Add ½ inch of water to the pot. Place a steamer, wire rack, plate, or the metal rings from mason jars in the bottom of the pot. (You need something to elevate the fish so that it isn't sitting in boiling water, but it doesn't need to be fancy.) Place the fish on top of the steamer and cover.

Place the pot on the stove and turn the heat to high. When the water starts boiling, lower the heat to a simmer. Cook, covered, for 4½ minutes per pound of fish. Turn off the heat, and let sit, covered, for 1 minute.

continued

Chinese-Style Steamed Fish with Ginger Sesame Sauce

continued

Check to see if the fish is fully cooked by poking a chopstick or knife through the thickest part. When it can pierce the flesh all the way through and the meat can lift off the bones with ease, the fish is cooked.

To serve, carefully transfer the fish from the pot to a platter. If you've split the fish, arrange its pieces back into its whole shape. Drizzle with shoyu, smother it generously in the ginger sesame sauce, stuffing some of the sauce into the fish slits, and serve immediately.

Ginger Sesame Sauce

Makes about 1¼ cup

2 bunches green onions, white and green parts, minced

1 bunch cilantro, minced

One 4-inch knob fresh ginger, finely minced

½ cup toasted sesame oil

2 teaspoons flaky sea salt

¾ cup olive oil

This sauce is bomb. I tell people it's like an Asian chimichurri that I use on everything from sashimi to rice to soup. Extra ginger sesame sauce can be stored in the fridge for up to 2 weeks.

In a medium bowl, combine the green onions, cilantro, ginger, sesame oil, and salt, and stir. (If you have a mortar and pestle, you can use it here instead.) In a small pot over medium-low heat, warm the olive oil for 3 minutes. Pour the warm olive oil over the green onion–cilantro mixture and stir. Taste and adjust the seasoning and reserve.

Garlicky Fish Piccata

Serves 4

1 pound boneless, skinless mū (bigeye bream or bigeye emperor fish), cut into 3 by 4-inch pieces

Flaky sea salt and freshly ground black pepper

All-purpose flour for dredging

6 tablespoons salted butter, plus more as needed

5 garlic cloves, chopped

¼ cup capers and their brine

¼ cup dry white wine (I prefer Chardonnay)

Juice of ½ lemon

Juice of ½ orange

Chopped fresh flat-leaf parsley for garnishing

Cooked, buttered pasta for serving

My dad didn't cook very much in our household, mainly because that was Mom's specialty that she did so well. But he did have a few dishes up his sleeve for the nights when he insisted my mom take a break; whenever he did proclaim his turn to throw down, we would beg him for chicken picante. Dad would butter-braise thick pieces of chicken breasts and add generous amounts of white wine, capers, and lemon juice. The kitchen would smell enticing as we asked on repeat if dinner was ready yet; like clockwork, my dad would always say, "I'll serve no wine until it's time!" Turns out what he actually was making was a delicious chicken piccata. He must've read a recipe somewhere long ago and remembered everything but the right name for it. So, during my entire upbringing, we fondly referred to this dish as Chicken Picante, completely unaware that "picante" means spicy and there's nothing spicy in it. But it's delicious. This quicker version uses fish instead of chicken.

Season the fish with salt and pepper. Dredge both sides of the fish in flour until fully coated.

In a large skillet over medium-high heat, melt 3 tablespoons of the butter. Working in batches, place the floured fish pieces in the skillet. Cook until the bottom side turns a nice golden brown, 3 to 4 minutes, then flip and repeat on the other side. Transfer the fish to a plate and cook the remaining pieces, adding more butter if needed.

Discard the butter in the skillet and wipe the skillet clean. Over medium-high heat, melt 2 tablespoons of the butter in the skillet. Add the garlic and cook for 1 to 2 minutes, stirring occasionally. When the garlic begins to brown, add the capers and their brine, wine, lemon juice, and orange juice, and stir. Let the sauce reduce for 2 minutes, then add the remaining 1 tablespoon of butter and stir until it melts. Pour the sauce over the fish fillets and garnish with parsley. Serve immediately with buttered pasta.

Fish Alternatives

Lingcod
Halibut
Rockfish

Dad's Baked Tomatoes

Serves 4 to 6

Olive oil for sautéing

¾ cup cooked, crumbled bacon or finely chopped Cured and Smoked Venison (page 97)

4 medium tomatoes

Flaky sea salt and freshly ground black pepper

3 garlic cloves, finely grated or microplaned

3 tablespoons salted butter

½ cup grated Parmigiano-Reggiano cheese

Chopped fresh flat-leaf parsley for garnishing

This recipe really shows me how innovative my dad was even when he didn't have much—a lesson I carry with me today. He created this one night when my mom was working the night shift and he was left to feed us. Aside from salad stuff—tomatoes, bacon bits, and some cheese—there wasn't much in the fridge. He whipped this up using jarred garlic and popped it in the toaster oven. These baked tomatoes smelled and tasted incredible; we devoured them all and would request his tomatoes again and again. My dad was so tickled that we loved it. These days, I like swapping in fresh garlic and our smoked venison, but home-cooked bacon bits also do the trick.

Preheat the oven to 400°F.

If you're using smoked venison: Line a plate with paper towels, or set a wire rack over a baking pan. In a medium skillet over medium-high heat, add enough olive oil to coat the bottom of the skillet, and warm the oil. Add the venison to the pan and cook until crisped, 2 minutes, stirring occasionally. Transfer the crisped venison to the prepared plate and reserve.

Slice the tomatoes in half horizontally. Place the tomato halves in a large ovenproof skillet, open-side up. Season with salt and pepper. Top each tomato half with the garlic and spread it across its face. Cut the butter into eight pieces and top each tomato half with a pat of butter, the bacon or venison, and the cheese. Bake in the oven until the tomatoes are soft and the cheese has turned golden brown, 25 to 30 minutes. Transfer the tomatoes to a serving platter, garnish with parsley, and serve.

Cooking with Fish and Wild Game

As you read this book, you're probably going to notice that it's a whole lot of fish and venison recipes. In fact, there's not a single chicken dish in this book. And it's not that I don't like chicken—I love chicken wings—it's just that over time, my cooking has evolved to using the ingredients I have on hand that connect me most to the natural world around me. I'm a spearfisher woman married to a gardening, bowhunting guy and surrounded by a community of fishermen and people who love to grow and harvest food. We live near the sea, and the neighboring islands, including my hometown of Maui, just so happen to be overrun with invasive axis deer.

The more I have taken the time to connect with the resources around me, the more I have seen the potential to work with them and elevate them in ways I haven't seen or tasted before. It became really hard for me to go out and buy chicken, beef, or pork from the grocery store when I have a freezer stocked with good animal protein where we know its source and the way it was harvested. So fish, venison, and veggies are what I eat and cook at home nowadays.

Most of these recipes have originated from great meals I tasted long ago that were made from store-bought ingredients (including my mom's). Over time, I have followed my curiosity to substitute as many local, wild ingredients as possible. It's fun for me. It's a way of truly honoring my harvests and sense of place. It also makes me feel cool and capable of preparing delicious and sometimes even fancy meals while sourcing them straight from land and sea. But if you are buying domestic or commercialized ingredients from the grocery store, please know that there is no shame in your game. These recipes are good recipes, plain and simple. They all work with wild game and will create spectacular meals, but if you have zero access to wild game, you can swap out whatever protein you do have and it's going to be a banger.

Venison and Mushroom Stroganoff

Serves 4 to 6

1½ pounds venison hindquarter or beef sirloin, sliced ⅛ inch thick against the grain

Flaky sea salt and freshly ground black pepper

Olive oil for sautéing

5 tablespoons salted butter

1 yellow onion, chopped

8 ounces button mushrooms, sliced

8 ounces oyster, chanterelle, or beech mushrooms, sliced (any medley of mushrooms will work)

2 garlic cloves, finely chopped

2 tablespoons all-purpose flour

3 tablespoons Dijon mustard

¾ cup dry white wine (I prefer Chardonnay)

2 cups water

1 tablespoon plus 1 teaspoon Better Than Bouillon Roasted Beef Base

1 cup sour cream

1 teaspoon Worcestershire sauce

I have no idea where my mom learned to cook beef stroganoff, but my dad and I loved her version and would request it all the time. Being the local Hawaiʻi family that we were, we ate it over white rice. Only later in life did I learn that people eat it over pasta noodles, but I still gravitate toward rice. I love making it now—an elevated version of so many of my favorite things: meat, mushrooms, and gravy.

Season the venison with salt and pepper. In a large skillet over high heat, add enough olive oil to coat the bottom of the skillet, and warm the oil. Working in batches, place the meat in the pan and sauté, while stirring, until just cooked through, about 1 minute. Transfer to a plate and reserve. Repeat for the remaining meat, adding more oil if necessary.

Add 3 tablespoons of butter to the skillet and lower the heat to medium-high. When the butter has melted, add the onion and stir, cooking until softened, about 2 minutes. Add all the mushrooms and stir to combine. Continue to cook, stirring occasionally, until the mushrooms have softened, about 5 minutes. Add the garlic, stir, and season with salt and pepper. Cook until touches of brown appear around the edges of the mushrooms and onion, and the pan is dry. Add the remaining 2 tablespoons butter and stir until melted, about 30 seconds, then sprinkle in the flour. Stir and cook for 1 minute. Add the mustard and stir to evenly coat the mushrooms and onion. Add the wine and stir, scraping any brown bits off the bottom of the skillet. Add the water and the beef bouillon base and stir thoroughly. When the liquid comes to a boil, lower the heat to a simmer. When the sauce begins to slightly thicken, about 15 minutes, add the cooked meat, sour cream, and Worcestershire sauce, and stir. Serve immediately.

Fish-Head Soup

Serves 6 to 8

One fish head from a 3- to 5-pound mū, gills and scales removed

5 ribs celery, chopped

4 carrots, scrubbed and chopped

2 beefsteak tomatoes, chopped

1 yellow onion, chopped

One 5-inch knob fresh ginger, peeled and sliced

2 garlic cloves, chopped

3 to 5 Hawaiian chiles or Thai chiles, chopped

Flaky sea salt and freshly ground black pepper

Shoyu for drizzling

Fish Alternatives

White seabass
Salmon
Yellowtail

My dad learned to make this version of fish soup from his Filipino fishing buddies. Dad is a big lumberjack-looking type of guy with big hands, and everything he cut was chunky—huge segments of onions, carrots, celery, and smashed garlic. But in no time, we'd have this spicy, clear fish-broth dinner on the table. It's so simple, so basic and I love the way it represents resourcefulness and getting the most out of the harvest. He'd often use the heads of papio, snapper, or nohu (a scorpionfish). When I make it, I use white-meat, silver-skinned fish—the kind from which you'd make sashimi or poke such as mū or yellowtail—for a clean, sweet-tasting broth.

Place the fish head in a large Dutch oven or a large wide pot. Add the celery, carrots, tomatoes, onion, ginger, garlic, and chiles. Season with salt and pepper and add enough water to cover by 1 inch. Cover the Dutch oven with a lid, bring to a boil over medium-high heat, then lower the heat to a simmer. After 20 minutes, remove the fish head and continue to cook the broth and veggies. When the fish head is cool enough to touch, scrape any meat scraps off the bones and reserve.

Cook until the veggies are soft, about 10 more minutes. Taste and adjust the seasoning. To serve, ladle the soup and veggies into bowls, and top with any reserved fish meat. Add the shoyu and serve.

Mū (Bigeye Bream or Bigeye Emperor)

Mū is a fish that most people haven't heard of, but it's my favorite reef fish to hunt. They're weird and they don't swim like normal fish—they seem to almost levitate. They are so smart and elusive. I need to turn into an underwater ninja to successfully land a mū—I can't make eye contact with them and I must lie completely still. They eat crustaceans and sea urchins and even have human-looking molars for teeth. Their diet makes their meat exceptionally sweet, and that's why this mysterious fish appears in so many of my recipes.

Lasagna

1 lb sausage or hamburger 1 1/2 tsp. salt
1 clove garlic, minced 1-1 lb. can tomatoes
1 Tbsp. basil 2-8 oz cans tomato sau
Brown meat, add rest of ing. simmer uncovere
30 min. Cook 10 oz lasagne noodles
Combine: 3 cups cottage cheese 2 beaten eggs
1/2 cup parmesan cheese 2 tsp. salt
2 Tbsp. parsley 1/2 tsp pepper
Slice 1 lb mozzarella cheese
Place 1/2 noodles, cheese + mozzarella + meat

in layers
Bake 375° 30 min
Let stand 10 min then serve

10-12 servings

Mom's Lasagna

Serves 6

10 to 12 dried lasagna noodles

¼ cup olive oil, plus more as needed

1½ pounds ground venison or ground beef (85 percent lean)

Flaky sea salt and freshly ground black pepper

1 medium yellow onion, diced

2 medium carrots, peeled and diced small

2 medium ribs celery, diced small

3 garlic cloves, minced

2 tablespoons dried oregano

1 tablespoon dried basil

⅔ cup dry red wine (I prefer Cabernet)

3 tablespoons tomato paste

One 14.5-ounce can diced tomatoes

One 15-ounce can tomato sauce

4 cups (32 ounces) whole-milk cottage cheese

½ cup finely grated Parmigiano-Reggiano cheese

3 eggs

⅔ cup minced fresh curly parsley

4 cups grated fresh mozzarella or white Cheddar cheese (about 1 pound)

Note: *This dish can be stored in the fridge for up to 3 days. Eat it cold (like I do when I'm starving), or heat up individual servings in a covered, lightly oiled cast-iron pan over medium heat.*

My mom always condemned store-bought marinara sauces. "They're too sweet!" she'd say as she added red wine to the pot of simmering red sauce and reiterated the importance of making her own. She also used cottage cheese instead of ricotta because "Ricotta is too expensive and no one will miss it." So, this is Mom's lasagna. It's got strict standards but also isn't trying too hard.

Preheat the oven to 375°F.

Bring a large pot of salted water to a boil over high heat. Add the lasagna noodles and cook according to the package directions. Drain the noodles in a colander and reserve.

Meanwhile, in a large skillet over medium-high heat, warm the olive oil. Once the oil is hot, add the venison, season with salt and pepper, and use a spatula to smash the meat down into one big patty. Cook until browned on one side, 4 to 5 minutes, then flip the meat over and let the other side brown, another 3 minutes. Using a wooden spoon, break up the meat, then add the onion, adding more oil if the skillet is dry. Gently stir, cooking until the onion starts to become translucent, about 4 minutes. Add the carrots and celery and stir to combine. After 3 minutes, add the garlic, oregano, and basil, and stir.

Lower the heat to medium, add the wine and tomato paste, and stir to combine. Add the diced tomatoes and the tomato sauce and stir.

Bring the sauce to a simmer, then lower the heat to low or medium-low and continue to cook for 15 minutes, stirring occasionally. Taste and adjust the seasoning and reserve.

In a medium mixing bowl, mix the cottage cheese with the Parmigiano-Reggiano cheese. Add the eggs and parsley and stir to combine. Add 2 teaspoons of salt and ½ teaspoon of pepper, then taste and adjust the seasoning.

To assemble the lasagna: Place a layer of noodles to cover the bottom of a 9 by 13-inch baking dish. Spoon half of the cottage cheese mixture onto the noodles and spread evenly over the top. Sprinkle with 2 cups of the mozzarella cheese. Next, spoon half of the meat sauce on top of the cheese, and spread evenly. Repeat the layering process with the remaining ingredients, finishing with sauce as the top layer.

Place the baking dish in the oven and bake for 30 minutes. Remove the lasagna from the oven and let stand for 10 minutes before cutting and serving.

Lobster Benedict

Serves 4 to 6

2 to 2½ pounds lobster tails, or 10 ounces thinly sliced Cured and Smoked Venison (page 97) or thinly sliced ham

Salted butter

Splash of white vinegar

8 eggs

4 English muffins, fork-split

Flaky sea salt

Paprika for garnishing (or cayenne pepper for a pop of spice)

Chopped flat-leaf parsley for garnishing

Hollandaise Sauce

8 tablespoons salted butter

3 egg yolks

2 tablespoons freshly squeezed lemon juice

Flaky sea salt

My favorite meal growing up was my mom's eggs Benedict. She was so tickled by how much I loved it that it became a classic dinner in our family. I grew up not knowing it was a breakfast food. Mom's hollandaise was so creamy and lemony that I always felt disappointed when I'd order eggs Benedict at restaurants. These days when I make Benedict, I swap out ham for either lobster or cured, smoked venison. But I will never change the hollandaise!

If using lobster tails: In a large pot, add 1 inch of water and the lobster tails and cover. Bring the water to a boil over medium-high heat, then turn down the heat to low and steam until the meat is opaque and firm, 7 to 8 minutes. Transfer the lobster tails to a platter to cool.

Make an incision running lengthwise on the underside of each lobster tail. Use your hands to crack open the shells and pull out the meat. If the lobster tail is a bigger one, use the heel of a knife to crack the top shell in several places before opening it. Thinly slice the lobster meat and reserve.

If using venison or ham: In a large pan over medium-high heat, add the venison or ham with a bit of butter and cook until it crisps up, about 4 minutes.

To make the sauce: In a small pan over medium-high heat, melt the butter. Once the butter is melted completely and bubbly, turn off the heat. In a blender, add the egg yolks and the lemon juice and a pinch of salt. Blend at medium-high speed until smooth, then slowly pour in the butter while the blender is running. Once everything is combined, turn off the blender and reserve.

To poach the eggs: In a small pot, add 4 inches of water and the vinegar. Bring the water to a boil over medium-high heat, then lower the heat to a gentle simmer. Crack one egg into a small bowl. Stir the water in the pot with a spoon in one direction to form a gentle vortex. Carefully slide the egg into the water in the middle of the vortex and cook until the egg white is set, about 3 minutes. With a slotted spoon, transfer the egg to a plate. Repeat with the remaining eggs.

To assemble: Toast the English muffins to the desired doneness and butter them. Top each muffin with the lobster meat and season with salt. Place a poached egg on top of each muffin, smother each egg in 2 tablespoons of hollandaise sauce, then dust with paprika. Serve immediately.

Grandma's Venison Ramen

Serves 4 to 6

2 pounds venison shoulder or pork butt, cut into large chunks

Coarse sea salt and freshly ground black pepper

¼ cup olive oil, plus more as needed

1 yellow onion, halved and cut into ¼-inch slices

12 cups water

One 4-inch knob fresh ginger, peeled and smashed (see Note)

¼ cup shoyu, plus more for seasoning

Three 9.5-ounce fresh ramen noodle packages

Toasted sesame oil

Toppings

6 eggs

Flaky sea salt

6 tablespoons salted butter

8 ounces king oyster (my preference) or button mushrooms, sliced

8 teaspoons chopped garlic (about 8 garlic cloves)

6 heads baby bok choy, ends trimmed

Shoyu

Toasted sesame oil for sautéing

6 green onions, white and green parts, chopped into 1-inch pieces

Dried wakame or roasted nori sheets, torn

Kimi's Kimchi (page 83), julienned

Crunchy Garlic Chili Oil (page 191; optional)

This dish is based on my grandma's style of home-cooked soup and Hawai'i's classic saimin. My grandma used to serve us soup with somen noodles and lots of toppings—the one that blew everyone's mind was always her braised, then crisped, garlicky pork. And in the long process of braising pork all day, she was also left with a pot of rich broth to fill our bowls.

I was eager to know if I could recreate my grandma's recipe using venison. Not only was I happy to discover that indeed I could, but it also solved the problem of how to use the tougher, sinewy cuts. Although they might become rubbery and chewy when cooked on fast, dry heat, braising them makes the sinew almost gelatinous, emulating the characteristics of a good, fatty piece of meat. This soup is the definition of home-cooked comfort. The majority of the cooking time for this recipe comes from simmering the broth for at least 3 hours, so plan accordingly. For a richly flavored broth, don't skip the step of browning the meat.

To make the broth and noodles: Generously season the venison with salt and pepper. Using a pot deep and wide enough to hold all the meat and broth, heat the olive oil over medium-high heat. Once the oil is hot and shimmering, add the venison pieces, working in batches. Let the venison brown for 5 to 6 minutes on one side before flipping it over; you want a nice brown bark to develop before flipping. Once all sides of the venison are browned, transfer the meat to a large plate and reserve. Add the onion to the pot (and more oil if needed), and sauté until browned, about 3 minutes, stirring occasionally. Add the water, the reserved meat, and the ginger to the pot. Stir, scraping any brown bits off the bottom of the pot, and bring to a boil. Turn down the heat to low, cover, and let simmer until the meat is fork-tender, about 3 hours. If too much water evaporates during simmering, add more to keep the meat submerged.

When the meat is tender, use tongs to transfer the meat and ginger to a cutting board. When the meat is cool enough to touch, chop it into 2-inch pieces and reserve. Discard the ginger. With a spoon, skim any foam or impurities off the top of the broth and discard. Add the shoyu and stir. Taste the broth, add more shoyu if needed, and reserve.

Bring a large pot of salted water to a boil. Add the ramen noodles and cook according to the package instructions. (Don't use any included flavor packets.) Drain the noodles in a colander. Drizzle sesame oil over the noodles, toss, and reserve.

continued

Grandma's Venison Ramen

continued

Note: *I use a mortar and pestle to smash ginger, but you can also use the base of a small pot.*

To cook the toppings: In a medium bowl, whisk the eggs and season with salt. In a large skillet over medium-high heat, melt 1 tablespoon of the butter. When the butter is bubbly, swirl the butter to coat the skillet. Add the eggs and turn the heat down to low. Let the eggs spread out on the pan into a flat egg sheet, as if making an omelet. As the eggs cook use a spatula to gently push their edges to the center to allow the runny parts to cook, tilting the skillet as necessary. When the egg is almost solid, flip it and cook the other side for another 30 seconds, then transfer it to a cutting board. Once the egg is cool enough to touch, roll it up like a jelly roll, slice it into ¼-inch ribbons, and reserve.

Wipe the skillet clean, then return it to the stove. Over medium-high heat, melt 3 tablespoons of the butter then add the mushrooms and cook without stirring until their edges begin to brown, 1½ minutes, then stir and flip the mushrooms and continue cooking until they turn soft, 4 minutes, stirring occasionally. Add 2 teaspoons of the minced garlic, stir, and continue cooking for 1 more minute. Season with salt and reserve.

In the same skillet over medium-high heat, melt the remaining 2 tablespoons of butter. Add the bok choy and stir to coat it evenly with the butter. Cover and cook for 4 minutes, stirring halfway through, then add 2 teaspoons of the garlic and continue to cook, uncovered, stirring occasionally. Let any excess liquid evaporate. When the skillet starts to get dry, add a drizzle of shoyu and turn off the heat. Stir once more, transfer the bok choy to a small dish, and reserve.

Wipe the skillet, then return it to the stove. Over medium-high heat, add enough sesame oil to coat the bottom of skillet and warm the oil. When the oil shimmers, add half of the venison. Sprinkle half of the green onions over the top of the meat and cook for 1 to 2 minutes. Flip the venison and sprinkle 2 teaspoons of the garlic over the top. Cook for another 1 to 2 minutes, then stir, letting the meat brown and form a crust. Drizzle some shoyu onto the meat, turn off the heat, and stir for 1 minute. Transfer the meat to a plate and reserve, then repeat with the remaining meat, green onions, 2 teaspoons garlic, and shoyu.

To serve: In a medium pot over medium-high heat, bring the broth to a simmer. Place all the toppings (egg, mushrooms, bok choy, venison, wakame, and kimchi) on serving plates. (I like to let the mushrooms and boy choy share a plate.) Using tongs or fingers, add a serving of noodles to each deep soup bowl. Let guests arrange their own toppings. (I encourage my guests to make their bowls pretty.) Ladle enough broth into each bowl until the noodles are submerged. Serve immediately with the garlic chili oil, if using.

Do Ahead: *The broth and the toppings can be made up to 1 day in advance and heated before serving.*

Smoked Shank Beans and Sopaipillas

Serves 8 to 10

Pinto Beans

2 pounds dried pinto beans

Olive oil for sautéing

1 yellow onion, chopped

2 garlic cloves, chopped

2 pounds smoked, bone-in ham hocks (see Note)

3 Hawaiian chiles or 1 seeded jalapeño or habanero chile, chopped

Flaky sea salt

Chile con Queso

3 tablespoons salted butter

½ yellow onion, finely chopped

2 garlic cloves, finely chopped

One 4-ounce can Hatch chiles, finely chopped

Flaky sea salt

2 tablespoons all-purpose flour

1½ cups half-and-half, plus more as needed

6 ounces sharp Cheddar cheese, grated

6 ounces mozzarella cheese, grated (not pre-grated because it will clump up)

Sopaipillas

4 cups all-purpose flour, plus more for dusting

¼ cup granulated sugar

1 tablespoon baking powder

Flaky sea salt

¼ cup salted butter, melted

1¼ cups whole milk

Neutral oil or lard for frying

Chili Pepper Water (page 34) or hot sauce of your choice for garnishing

continued

Dad loves beans. This savory, smoky dish is part of his family roots in New Mexico. Mom learned to cook it to perfection as a way to say "I love you," and I was an instant fan of this cowboy comfort food. She'd always make a huge pot of beans and serve it with chili pepper water and a spicy chile con queso. She'd fry sopaipillas, a rustic, doughy bread that can be served sweet but in our case was always savory. We'd bite them open and fill the hollow center with beans and the thick broth. It was hearty and comforting, and the next day it would get even better.

This recipe makes a lot of food, but Mom cooked beans in a huge batch because we'd want a bowl of them for two days in a row (but it works well for a gathering too). On the third day, Mom would heat up the leftover beans and mix in the chile con queso in a cast-iron pan. The heat would reduce what was left of the thick, collagen-filled broth, and the starchy pintos would break down into a mush until we basically had some bomb refried beans. She would wrap them in flour tortillas with cheese and freeze the burritos so we always had a quick meal when needed. Keep in mind, this recipe calls for an overnight soak time on the beans!

To make the pinto beans: Place the dried beans in a large pot and add enough water to cover by 3 inches. Cover the pot with a lid and let soak overnight. Drain the beans, rinse with water, and reserve.

In a large pot over medium-high heat, add enough olive oil to coat the bottom of the pot, and warm the oil. Add the onion and stir, cooking until it begins to soften, about 2 minutes. Add the garlic and stir. After 4 minutes, add the ham hocks, chiles, beans, and 2 teaspoons salt. Add enough water to cover the beans by 1 inch. Bring to a boil, then turn down the heat to low, cover, and let simmer until the beans are soft and the meat is fork-tender, about 2 hours. Taste and season with salt and reserve. (In my family, we ladled the beans and their broth into individual bowls and anyone who wanted some of the meat could add some to their bowl using tongs. You could also take the meat off the bone, chop it up, and add the meat back to the beans.)

To make the chile con queso: In a medium saucepan over medium-high heat, melt the butter. Add the onion and garlic, stir, and cook until they turn soft, about 2 minutes. Add the chiles and a pinch of salt, stir, then cook for about 3 minutes. Add the flour, stir to thoroughly incorporate, and cook for 1 minute, then turn the heat to low. Slowly drizzle in the half-and-half while

Smoked Shank Beans and Sopaipillas

continued

Note: *Any smoked meat will work here, but smoked meat on a bone, like venison shanks, is even better. You can also smoke the meat yourself. If you're smoking venison shanks, season them with salt and pepper and smoke them at 200°F for 3 to 5 hours.*

you stir. When it's incorporated, cook for 2 minutes, stirring occasionally. Turn the heat to medium-low and then add the Cheddar and mozzarella cheeses, stirring occasionally until melted. If the mixture looks a little thick, add another splash of half-and-half. When the chile con queso has reached the desired consistency, turn off the heat. Taste and season with salt and reserve.

About 1 hour before serving, make the sopaipillas: Lightly flour a clean work surface. In a large bowl, add the flour, sugar, baking powder, and 1¼ teaspoons of salt, and whisk to combine. Add the melted butter and stir to combine, then add the milk. Using your hands, form the dough into a shaggy ball, transfer to the floured work surface, then knead until smooth, about 2 minutes. Divide the dough into four balls, then cover the dough balls with a damp kitchen towel and let sit for 20 minutes.

Dust a work surface with flour. Roll out one of the dough balls into a super-thin rectangle about 11 by 11 inches long and ⅛ inch thick. Cut the slab on the diagonal into 3-inch-wide ribbons, then cut on the diagonal in the opposite direction into 4-inch-wide ribbons to make diamond-shaped pieces. Repeat with the remaining dough balls.

Place a wire rack over a baking pan and set near the stove. In a large, heavy skillet, add 1 inch of oil and heat over high heat until hot, about 3 minutes. Working in batches, gently place the diamond-shaped dough pieces into the oil, cook on one side until golden brown, about 1 minute, and then flip and cook the other side, 1 minute more. (The dough should puff up. If it doesn't, make sure the dough is rolled thin enough and the oil is hot enough.) When the sopaipillas are nicely browned, transfer to the prepared wire rack to cool. Sprinkle with salt and reserve.

To serve: Over medium-low heat, warm the chile con queso. Place large serving bowls of warm pinto beans and chile con queso alongside a platter of freshly fried sopaipillas. Garnish with chili pepper water or hot sauce.

2

My Travels

Recipes from Oceans and Friends Around the World

In my twenties, I went from being a full-time line cook to a part-time art teacher to a full-time starving artist. I was literally painting fish on trucker hats and posting my creations for sale on social media for twenty-five bucks each. To most of my friends, family, and even myself at times, it looked like I was moving backwards in life, but I was finding a way to dive more often. And I noticed that by sharing photos of my recent catches from my dives, a community was forming online of people who supported me and would actually buy my hand-painted hats.

I struggled every month to make rent, but I had the freedom and flexibility to pick up and run to the ocean when the seas were calm and the waves were down. I saved money on groceries by growing a garden as well as harvesting from the sea. And as I did, I got better and better at diving. Soon, I started getting job offers based around doing my craft underwater. These gigs started locally but then led to international opportunities. The stress of paying rent and bills every month lessened as these opportunities escalated, but even more importantly to me, I was able to pursue diving and TRAVEL! I never realized I could have both sides of that coin—more stable paychecks while doing my passion.

Freediving and spearfishing literally gave me the world. The travel assignments came in a colorful assortment of jobs: TV shows, photo shoots, scientific expeditions, and product testing for outdoor brands. The more I traveled and worked, the more work I got offered to travel. For about a decade, I was often abroad more than I was home, and I said "yes" to it all.

I got to explore all seven continents and the oceans around them—and taste the food along the way! From overcoming my fear of the unknown whenever diving somewhere new to simply walking through local markets and being mesmerized by the intriguing ingredients available, traveling breathed life into every ounce of me. Sharing a meal with friends from entirely different cultures and backgrounds was a sacred celebration that fed my soul with love that stayed with me long after I left.

I get to take those memories with me, see the world a little differently, and forever become a part of those experiences. When I take a bite of creamy, coconutty poisson cru, I can smell the sweet air of Tahiti. When I slowly stew a pot of seafood, wine, and sausage to make a cocimiento, I'm back wholeheartedly laughing and tipsy with the local waitresses I took on a swim-out shore dive in Chile. These recipes are from and for the people who showed me love through my travels, and no matter how short our time together or long it's been since then, I fondly see them again whenever I make these meals.

Top: It all starts with the birds.
Bottom: Dan Malloy trying to eat his sandwich.

Poisson Cru

(Creamy Coconut Ceviche)

Serves 4 to 6

1 pound boneless, skinless fish fillet from any mild-flavored fish that can be eaten raw (see page 20), such as ono (wahoo)

3 mini or 1 English cucumber, peeled, seeded, and diced small

2 tomatoes, seeded and coarsely chopped

1 red, yellow, or orange bell pepper, diced small

1 carrot, peeled and grated

½ yellow onion, diced small

½ bunch cilantro, coarsely chopped

1½ teaspoons flaky sea salt

Juice of 3 limes

Juice of ½ orange

Two 13.5-ounce cans unsweetened coconut milk

Just the thought of this dish sweeps me away to the many dive trips I've experienced in French Polynesia. The sweet smells of tiaré blossoms in the air, monoï (roasted coconut oil) on my skin, and a cold Hinano beer in hand and a bowl of poisson cru after having spent all day in the ocean. Damn. Take me back. *Poisson* is French for "fish" and *cru* means "coconut." Those are the key players of this fabulous creation, but all the veggies married together between them form a rainbow of both colors and flavors that make you feel as light and vibrant as the ingredients themselves. Poisson cru is great over a bowl of brown rice, nice with chips, and truly divine just eaten straight up with a spoon.

With a sharp knife, cut the fish into small cubes roughly ⅓-inch wide. In a large mixing bowl, combine the fish, cucumbers, tomatoes, bell pepper, carrot, onion, cilantro, salt, lime juice, and orange juice. Stir to combine. Pour in the coconut milk and mix until thoroughly combined. Chill in the fridge for at least 1 hour to let the flavors develop, but if you are out of time, serve immediately.

Fish Alternatives

Uhu (parrotfish)
White seabass
Tuna

Green Papaya Salad

Serves 2 to 4

One 1- to 1½-pound green papaya, hard and green on the outside with no yellow spots

1 cup roasted, unsalted peanuts or cashews

¼ cup dried shrimp

1 tablespoon granulated sugar

1 habanero chile, roughly chopped (or more!)

1 garlic clove

3 tablespoons fish sauce

Juice of 1 lime

4 ounces green beans, trimmed and cut into 1-inch pieces (about 1 cup)

1 cup cherry tomatoes, halved

Chopped fresh cilantro for garnishing

Lime wedges for garnishing

Growing up in Hawai'i, I always thought of papaya as a soft, sweet fruit, but during my first time in Thailand, I remember being absolutely amazed as I walked through the streets and saw vendors selling green papaya salad from their pushcarts. They would make it right in front of me with their mortar and pestle, asking, "How spicy? One, two, three, or four chiles?" I remember it tasting so fresh and crunchy, with green beans, tomatoes, salt, and spice. It opened my mind to fruit like mango and papaya not being served ripe. Alongside making fresh, ripe sweet-fruit breakfasts, I now pick them green for salads too.

Use a vegetable peeler to peel the skin off the papaya, then cut the papaya in half. If there are seeds, scrape them out with a spoon and discard. Using either a mandoline on the julienne setting or a slice peeler, shred the papaya into long strips. (You can also use a knife and cut the papaya into julienne strips.)

Use a mortar and pestle to roughly crush the nuts. (Or use a knife to finely chop.) Reserve.

Place the shrimp, sugar, habanero, and garlic in the mortar and pestle. Crush until well combined. Add the fish sauce and lime juice and stir until the sugar dissolves. Pour the mixture into a large bowl.

Use the mortar and pestle to bruise the green beans (or smash with the side of a chef's knife), then add the pieces to the bowl.

Add the papaya slivers to the bowl, crushing and bruising them with your hands. Squeeze the tomatoes in your hands over a sink to remove the seeds, then place them in the bowl. Toss the salad with your hands. Add half of the nuts and toss again. Divide the salad onto plates and garnish with cilantro, lime wedges, and the rest of the nuts.

Furikake Salmon

Serves 4 to 6

1½ pounds skin-on salmon fillet, cut into 4 to 6 portions

Flaky sea salt and freshly ground black pepper

¾ cup mayonnaise

2 teaspoons citrus zest (lemon, lime, orange, or a combination of any)

1 tablespoon freshly squeezed citrus juice (lemon, lime, or orange)

¼ cup furikake

Lemon wedges for squeezing

Shoyu for drizzling

When I was a teenager, every summer my family and I would travel to Alaska to go salmon fishing. My dad ended up buying land and building some cabins in southeast Alaska because he fell in love with the fishing so much. To this day, when I go to my dad's cabins, it's fun to bring our local flavors from home, like Japanese furikake seasoning, and make a quick and easy recipe. There's just something so simple, yet magical, that happens when crunchy, salty furikake and broiled mayo melt together into an omega-3–rich fish fillet. Yum! When I make it, I like to think of it as frosting a cake, with the fillet being the cake, the mayonnaise as the frosting, and the furikake as the sprinkles to finish. Stick a candle in it and I'll take this for my birthday any day!

Preheat the oven to 450°F.

Season the skinless, fleshy side of the salmon portions with salt and pepper—no need to season the skin. In a medium bowl, combine the mayo, citrus zest, and citrus juice. Mix until combined. Generously slather the mayonnaise mixture onto the nonskin side of the seasoned salmon (at least 3 tablespoons on each fillet), spreading it as evenly as possible. Sprinkle furikake on top of the mayonnaise-covered salmon, about 2 teaspoons for each portion.

Place the salmon on a baking sheet. Cook in the oven until the thickest part of the fillet is cooked all the way through, 12 to 14 minutes. Test the salmon for doneness by poking the thickest part with a chopstick or fork; you should be able to pierce the flesh easily all the way through. Set the oven to broil on high heat, move the salmon to the top rack, and continue to cook until the mayonnaise mixture begins to brown, about 1 minute. Serve the salmon immediately with a squeeze of lemon and a drizzle of shoyu.

Fish Alternatives

Swordfish
Tautog (blackfish)
Black cod

Citrusy Ceviche with Avocado

Serves 4 to 6

¾ pound any boneless, skinless, white-meat fish (like snapper) that you can eat raw (see page 20), cut into small dice

2 cups roughly chopped, seeded tomatoes

2 peeled, seeded miniature cucumbers or 1 English cucumber, finely diced

1 red, orange, or yellow bell pepper, finely diced

½ large yellow or red onion, finely diced

Kernels cut from one ear of corn (about 1 cup; optional)

¾ cup roughly chopped fresh cilantro

2 ribs celery, finely diced

¾ cup freshly squeezed lime juice

⅓ cup freshly squeezed orange juice

¼ cup freshly squeezed lemon juice

2 tablespoons ketchup

2½ teaspoons fine sea salt

Hot sauce

Minced fresh serrano, jalapeño, or Hawaiian chiles (optional)

1 ripe avocado, cut into thin slices or diced

Tortilla chips for serving (optional)

I learned to make ceviche on Maui as a kid. José, one of my dad's employees from Mexico, taught me this recipe. But I consider this a travel dish not only because of the delicious versions I've eaten in Mexico and Peru, but also because it's a recipe I've carried with me everywhere. It comes in especially handy on live-aboard boat trips because I don't need a fire or a kitchen. I know that as long as I can pack a cooler with fresh veggies and citrus, all I need is a cutting board and a sharp knife. Every time we get the first fish in the boat, I'll make the ceviche and by the end of the day, it's perfect with spoons or tortilla chips with some beers on the side. A sidenote on the celery: Dicing it small is important so that it doesn't overpower this dish's texture and flavor.

In a large mixing bowl, add the fish, tomatoes, cucumbers, bell pepper, onion, corn, cilantro, and celery. Stir to combine. Add the lime juice, orange juice, lemon juice, ketchup, and salt and stir. Season with hot sauce and chiles, if using. Transfer the ceviche to a large serving bowl. Top with or gently fold in the avocado. Serve with tortilla chips or enjoy as is!

Do Ahead: *This ceviche can be made up to 1 day in advance and stored, covered, in the fridge.*

Fish Alternatives

Marlin
Triggerfish
Rockfish

Fins of Gold:
A Story of Spearing ʻAhi

April 2017—Isla Secas, Panama

It all starts with the birds. When the right ones are circling above, they become guiding indicators that the baitfish will soon be pushed up to the surface by the predators below. When the water starts roiling and the birds start diving, the buffet is officially open and the feeding frenzy starts.

We are always last in line for the feast. I jump into the water, but the action has just ended and I've missed the event completely. But still, the signs are everywhere. Scales glittering in the water are all that remain of the bait ball that was just here. But the birds above are reorganizing. These clues guide us to the next feast.

This is the game we've played all morning. The hardest part for me is containing all the adrenaline and energy that comes with timing my dives in order to descend to the depths and find what I'm looking for. My friends on the boat keep watching the birds, and there's such urgency in their voices as they shout directions at me.

Then I hear the dolphins. They approach me on the surface and seem to be slowly reorganizing themselves for the next hunt. "May I swim with you?" I legitimately ask them with my mind. And I feel instantly calmer as I watch the pod swim. But, as I swim with them, I only stare below into the darkness. I know what's down there; I just don't know exactly where or how deep. The momentum builds and the pod seems energized and ready to strike. I swear I hear it—the screaming from within, the screaming from the boat, from the birds, from the dolphins—"Dive now! Dive now! Dive now!!"

There's no time to second-guess or even prepare. I take a breath, leave the dolphins, and drop into the darkness. I sink further into the murk, which never feels comfortable. I can't see. Keep going. I keep sinking. When I finally start to break and consider turning back, I see gold. Sickles and flashes of gold everywhere! It is the most surreal and invigorating feeling just to see them. I'm now surrounded by an army so thick, but my focus heightens immediately as I know I've come to lock in on just one fish.

RIFFE

KEEP WILD Co

The Whole Lobster Bisque

Serves 4 to 6

3 pounds shell-on whole lobster or lobster tails
Coarse sea salt and freshly ground black pepper
¼ cup salted butter
1 yellow onion, chopped
2 carrots, scrubbed and chopped
2 ribs celery, finely chopped
3 garlic cloves, chopped
¼ cup all-purpose flour
2 ripe beefsteak tomatoes, seeded and chopped, or one 15-ounce can chopped tomatoes
¼ cup tomato paste
Splash of white wine (I prefer Chardonnay)
Juice of ½ lemon
2 dried bay leaves
½ cup heavy cream
2 pinches ground nutmeg
Chopped fresh flat-leaf parsley for garnishing

Note: *Excess lobster stock can be stored in the freezer for up to 6 months.*

On a dive trip in the Bahamas with my friend Steve Rinella, dive mentor Cam Kirkconnell, and two of the most badass freediving cinematographers, Perrin James and my husband, Justin—God, what a crew!—the lobsters were so abundant. As we processed our hefty harvest, I took all the shells and heads and started making my stock. It was hot and the kitchen felt like a furnace. Everyone thought I was crazy, but when I served a lunch of lobster bisque with a side of lobster-meat grilled cheese sandwiches, we were all happy kids again.

Add the lobster to a large pot of water with a pinch of salt. Cover and bring to a boil over medium-high heat, then turn down the heat to medium-low and simmer for 15 minutes if using a whole lobster or 10 minutes if using tails. Using tongs, transfer the lobster to a large bowl to cool. Turn off the heat and reserve the liquid. If using a whole lobster, break off the legs, then use kitchen shears to cut the joints off each end of the legs. Use a chopstick to poke as much meat out as you can from the legs and cavity of the lobster. Reserve the shells. Break the tail off, and use the heel of a knife to crack the top shell of the tail in several places. Flip the tail and cut lengthwise on the underside. Use your hands to crack open the shell and pull out the tail meat. Chop all of the lobster meat into bite-size pieces and reserve.

Put the shells back in the pot of water, add more water if necessary to cover them, and then cover the pot with a lid. Bring to a boil over medium-high heat, then turn the heat to low and simmer for 35 minutes. Drain the liquid from the shells, discard the shells, and reserve the stock.

Meanwhile, in a separate large pot over medium-high heat, melt the butter. Add the onion, carrots, and celery, and cook, stirring occasionally. After 4 minutes, add the garlic, stir, and continue to cook. When the veggies become soft, another 6 minutes, add the flour and stir. Mix in the tomatoes and the tomato paste. Add the wine and stir, scraping any bits off the bottom of the pot. Add 6 cups of the reserved lobster stock, the lemon juice, and bay leaves, and cook for 12 minutes, stirring occasionally. Season with salt and pepper. Remove the bay leaves and let the mixture cool slightly.

Working in batches, pour the solids and liquid into a blender. (Fill your blender to half capacity per batch as this will be hot.) Blend on medium speed until smooth and transfer the blended bisque to a large bowl. Repeat with the remaining solids and liquid, and pour the bisque back into the large pot on the stove. Over medium-high heat, add the heavy cream and nutmeg to the bisque and stir. Season with salt and pepper. Divide the lobster meat into bowls and ladle the bisque over the meat. Garnish with parsley and serve immediately.

Lettuce Wraps with Tangy Fish Sauce

Serves 4 to 6

Tangy Fish Sauce

2 tablespoons water

2 tablespoons fish sauce

2 tablespoons granulated sugar

1 tablespoon freshly squeezed lime juice

1 teaspoon white vinegar

1 garlic clove, minced

Minced fresh hot chiles (optional)

Filling

Olive oil for sautéing

1 pound ground mutton, venison, or lean beef

½ yellow onion, finely chopped

½ cup grated carrots

½ cup chopped green onions, white and green parts

½ cup finely chopped cooking greens, such as collards, spinach, or cabbage

¼ cup finely chopped fresh cilantro stems

2 garlic cloves, minced

1 tablespoon shoyu

1 tablespoon fish sauce

Juice of 1 lime

For serving

1 small head butter lettuce, leaves separated, or 1 bunch collard greens with stems removed

2 mini cucumbers, sliced lengthwise into thin strips

½ cup fresh mint leaves

½ cup fresh cilantro leaves

Lime wedges

This recipe celebrates my travels throughout Southeast Asia, where I fell in love with the copious amounts of fresh herbs and vegetables in every meal. These wraps leave me feeling so satisfied, yet light, and the bold flavors of citrus and fish sauce make my taste buds dance in delight. They also hold up perfectly to even the gamiest of wild game.

To make the sauce: In a small bowl, combine the water, fish sauce, sugar, lime juice, vinegar, garlic, and chiles (if using). Stir to combine until the sugar dissolves, and reserve.

To make the filling: In a large skillet over medium-high heat, add enough olive oil to coat the bottom of the skillet. Add the mutton and use a spatula to smash the meat down into one big patty. Cook until browned, 4 to 5 minutes, then flip the meat over and let the other side brown, another 3 minutes. Using a wooden spoon, break up the meat, then add the onions, adding more oil if the skillet is dry. (When cooking lean meats like sheep or venison, sometimes you need extra oil.) After 2 minutes, add the carrots, green onions, chopped greens, cilantro stems, and garlic, and stir to combine. When all the veggies have softened, about 5 minutes, add the shoyu, fish sauce, and lime juice, and stir. Continue to cook for 1 more minute, then turn off the heat and transfer the mixture into a small serving bowl.

To serve: Arrange the lettuce leaves, cucumbers, mint, cilantro, lime wedges, and tangy fish sauce on a platter along with the bowl of ground mutton mixture. Assemble the lettuce wraps by scooping the ground mutton mixture into the lettuce leaves along with your desired mix of toppings (cucumber, mint, cilantro, and a squeeze of lime) and a spoonful of the tangy fish sauce.

Korean-Style Pancakes

Serves 4 to 6

Pancakes

2 cups all-purpose flour

2 cups water

2 eggs

2 teaspoons flaky sea salt

Freshly ground black pepper

2 cups thinly sliced zucchini (matchstick-size)

1 cup grated carrots

4 ounces king oyster mushrooms, cut into thin strips

1 bunch green onions, white and green parts, cut into 2-inch pieces

¼ yellow onion, thinly sliced

Neutral oil for frying

Dipping Sauce

½ cup shoyu

¼ cup rice vinegar

3 tablespoons Crunchy Garlic Chili Oil (page 191)

1 green onion, white and green parts, chopped

1 tablespoon toasted sesame oil

White sesame seeds for garnishing

I started cooking veggie pancakes after spending time in Korea with the haenyeo (the female divers of the Jeju province). I got the opportunity to dive with them when I was seven months pregnant and to learn their perspective on motherhood. The haenyeo told me of the hardships they had to endure—they had to row their boats to other islands to get diapers for their babies, and they laughed at me when I asked them about drinking coffee while pregnant. What a luxury—they couldn't afford coffee! Despite these difficulties, as long as they could have their small gardens and grow food, they always ate well, making pancakes like these from whatever was in their yard and elevating vegetables to something special. In the United States, pancakes are sweet and vegetables are salad. But I love the way these savory pancakes are made from a whole medley of veggies that are all in one bite alongside a delicious dipping sauce.

To make the pancakes: In a large bowl, add the flour, water, eggs, and salt, and stir to combine. Season with pepper. Add the zucchini, carrots, mushrooms, green onions, and yellow onion, and stir to combine.

In a large skillet over medium-high heat, warm enough oil to coat the bottom of the skillet. Working in batches, add 1½ cups of the veggie mixture to the skillet and spread it out with a spatula. When the pancake has developed a crispy texture with some brown edges, 3 to 4 minutes, flip it and repeat on the other side. Transfer the pancake to a plate or platter and repeat with the remainder of the batter. Adjust the heat and add more oil as needed.

To make the dipping sauce: In a medium bowl, add the shoyu, rice vinegar, garlic chili oil, green onion, and sesame oil. Stir to combine and garnish with the sesame seeds.

Cut the pancakes into wedges and serve alongside the dipping sauce.

Kimi's Kimchi

Yields 1½ quarts

1 large head Napa cabbage, coarsely chopped into 2-inch pieces

Fine sea salt

2 carrots, peeled and cut into a 2-inch julienne

1 bunch green onions, white and green parts, cut into 1-inch pieces

One 3-inch knob fresh ginger, peeled and minced

4 garlic cloves, finely grated

Juice of 2 unpeeled Fuji apples or 1¼ cups unfiltered apple juice

½ cup gochugaru (Korean chili flakes), plus more as needed

¼ cup fish sauce

¼ cup maple syrup

When I visited Korea, I ate my weight in kimchi. I loved how every restaurant I dined at served their own homemade version, some more spicy, some more pungent, but they were always a staple. When I came back home, I started experimenting. I like to use a ceramic kimchi crock, but you can use a wide-mouth jar or bowl. Heads-up, this recipe takes at least 3 days before it's ready to serve.

In a large mixing bowl, add the cabbage and 3½ tablespoons of the salt. Mix with your hands, massaging the salt into the cabbage leaves for about 1 minute. Add the carrots, green onions, ginger, garlic, apple juice, gochugaru, fish sauce, and maple syrup, and toss to mix. Taste and season with salt and gochugaru.

Transfer the cabbage mixture to a large crock or a wide-mouth jar (at least 32 ounces) and push it down with your hands to pack it tightly, leaving at least 1 inch of headspace. If you have a weight or a small plate that fits in the crock, put it on top of the cabbage to make sure the cabbage stays submerged in the liquid. Cover the crock with a cloth. Use a rubber band to tighten the cloth around the jar opening. Let the kimchi sit at room temperature for 3 days. Check on it every day and press it down to keep it submerged in the liquid. Skim off any white, milky residue that collects on the surface. If you're using a weight, clean off any residue. (This residue is harmless and not a sign that the kimchi has spoiled. It's also normal for the kimchi to show signs of bubbling and fermenting.) Transfer the kimchi to a clean jar, cover, and refrigerate. It's ready to eat, but it will continue to ferment and develop in flavor for 3 to 4 weeks, stored in the fridge.

Thai Veggie Curry

Serves 4 to 6

2 tablespoons coconut oil
½ yellow onion, chopped
2 ribs celery, chopped
1 orange, yellow, or red bell pepper, chopped
1 large carrot, scrubbed and chopped
1 Japanese eggplant, chopped
8 ounces button mushrooms, chopped
1 cup 1-inch pieces green long beans or green beans
½ zucchini, chopped
2 garlic cloves, minced
3 tablespoons red curry paste (I prefer the Mae Ploy brand)
Two 13.5-ounce cans unsweetened coconut milk
1 cup julienned canned bamboo shoots
1 cup canned baby corn
½ cup water
2 tablespoons fish sauce
1 tablespoon maple syrup
½ cup coarsely chopped or torn Thai basil
¼ cup coarsely chopped fresh cilantro
Mango chutney for garnishing (optional)

My first time in Thailand was with a group of girlfriends from Oahu who I've known since my early twenties. We scraped and saved every penny we could to afford that trip. We snorkeled around vibrant reefs and trekked in the jungle and stayed with hill tribes in simple shacks. And boy, did we eat! I was blown away by Thai cuisine but especially in awe when I got to Chiang Mai and tasted an abundance of fresh vegetables and bold spices. I ate veggie curries for breakfast, lunch, and dinner. It's something I'll continue to make for the rest of my life. Go ahead and add protein if you want, but it's already so flavorful and satisfying as it is.

In a large pot over medium-high heat, warm the coconut oil. Stir in the onion and celery and cook for 1 minute. Add the bell pepper, carrot, eggplant, mushrooms, and beans, stir, and cook for 5 minutes. Stir in the zucchini and garlic and cook for 1 minute. Stir in the red curry paste and cook for 2 minutes. Stir in the coconut milk, then stir in the bamboo shoots and baby corn. Add the water, fish sauce, and maple syrup. Bring to a boil, then turn down the heat to medium-low, cover, and let simmer until the veggies are softened but still firm, about 15 minutes. Stir in the Thai basil and cilantro. Serve while warm with the mango chutney.

Riffe

Paulo's Polvo à Lagareiro

(Roasted Octopus with Olive Oil and Smashed Potatoes)

Serves 6 to 8

When I was thirty, my childhood best friend, Tawny, tragically passed in a car accident. After she died, I flew to Maui to help clean out her room. Buried in the bottom of a drawer, I found a paper with her handwriting on it: "What would you want to do more?" *Travel,* she wrote. "Whose life would you want to emulate?" *Kimi's,* she wrote. And then the third one: "Where would you want to go?" *The Azores.* I had never heard of the Azores but I looked them up and immediately saw images of a beautiful chain of islands that looked very similar to Hawai'i, but in the Atlantic Ocean off the coast of Portugal. I promised myself that one day I would take her there in spirit.

A few years later, Riffe International—the company that makes all my spearguns and freediving equipment—invited me on a trip to Pico Island in the Azores to dive with fellow Riffe-sponsored spearfisher and Azorean Paulo Afonso Vieira.

I immediately said "Yes!" I had known of Paulo and the huge fish he landed, but my mind went straight to Tawny. She was obsessed with seashells, and right before she passed, I had just found a jackpot of Hawai'i's most sought-after ones—sunrise shells. I was so excited to surprise Tawny with this mother lode of sunnies for Christmas, but I was never able to give them to her because she died in October. So I packed up my sunrise shells for Tawny and headed to the Azores to bring her there.

I can't believe it is possible to travel halfway across the globe and meet somebody who has the exact same passions, interests, and way of life. Paulo and I bonded over our love for the ocean, our views on sustainability, and our dream of living a simple life with great food. We went diving for lapas (Portuguese limpets), spent time at his dad's peach orchard and his mom's garden, foraged for the freshest ingredients, and walked down cobblestone roads with freshly baked bread and bottles of wine to go with it.

On the last day of the trip, Paulo took me to a spot to get lapas; the underwater structure was stunning. I knew this is where I would give Tawny her shells. Right before I got in the water, I told Paulo about Tawny and the sunrise shells. When I opened my hand to show them to him, he looked like he had seen a ghost. He said, "Vieira, those shells are me." Confused, I asked, "What do you mean? These are sunrise shells and they are found only in Hawai'i." He laughed and said, "They are also called Vieira. That's my family name." I was stunned when Paulo later gave me Vieiras because they are practically a twin of our sacred sunrise shells. That day, when I left my sunrise shells for Tawny, I realized that this trip wasn't just about me bringing Tawny to the Azores, but she was literally bringing *me* there to meet Paulo, a new lifelong friend.

This remains one of the most special trips of my life, and everything tasted really good. Like that special kind of good where even the wine and the salt in the air are extra delicious. I asked Paulo to share his octopus recipe he cooked for me. I tried it back in Hawai'i and damn, it takes me right back. Obrigado, Paulo. Love you, Tawny.

continued

Paulo's Polvo à Lagareiro

continued

Potatoes

1½ pounds tiny potatoes (1 to 2 inches)

Flaky sea salt

⅓ cup diced mild Portuguese sausage or Spanish chorizo

2 tablespoons chopped fresh rosemary

Olive oil for drizzling

Octopus

One 3-pound octopus, previously frozen for at least 24 hours and defrosted (see Note)

2 tablespoons coarse sea salt

1 yellow onion, peeled and left whole

1½ cups dry white wine (I prefer Chardonnay)

2 cups olive oil

12 garlic cloves, smashed with the peels on

½ red or orange bell pepper, seeded and cut into thin strips

2 large jalapeño chiles, Anaheim chiles, or other mild chiles of your choice, seeded and cut into long, thin strips

Flaky sea salt for seasoning

Crusty sliced bread for serving

Note: *If you have fresh octopus, gut it by pulling the head inside out and removing the innards. Freeze the octopus in a resealable bag or covered container for at least 4 days to tenderize it before defrosting.*

Preheat the oven to 450°F.

To make the potatoes: Bring a large pot of salted water and the potatoes to a boil over medium-high heat. Turn down the heat to medium-low and let simmer until the potatoes can be pierced with a knife or chopstick, about 10 minutes. Meanwhile, lightly oil a baking sheet and set aside. Drain the potatoes, then place them on a cutting board or plate. Using your closed fist or the bottom of a heavy drinking glass, give each potato a punch to smash and flatten it to roughly ¼ inch thick (they should be somewhat irregular). Place them, dented side up, on the prepared baking sheet. Season with salt. Sprinkle with the Portuguese sausage and rosemary and drizzle with olive oil. Place the baking sheet in the oven and cook until the potatoes are golden brown and crispy, 18 to 20 minutes. Remove from the oven and reserve.

To make the octopus: Place the defrosted octopus in a large mixing bowl and sprinkle with the salt. Use your hands to vigorously squeeze, push, and press the entire octopus for 7 minutes—think of it as a deep tissue massage. At the thicker parts of the legs and head, apply pressure as you squeeze. Thoroughly rinse the octopus in cold running water. It will foam somewhat; keep rinsing until all the suds are gone and the water runs clear.

Place the cleaned octopus in the pot of an electric pressure cooker. Add the onion and wine. Lock the lid into place and cook on high pressure for 14 minutes. Manually release the pressure. (Alternatively, cook the octopus on a stovetop: In a medium pot over medium-high heat, add the octopus, onion, wine, and 1½ cups water. Bring to a boil, then turn down the heat to medium-low, cover, and let simmer for 1 hour.)

When the steam has released from the pressure cooker, remove the lid and pierce the thickest part of the octopus with a wooden chopstick or fork to make sure it punctures easily. If it's not done, put it back in the pressure cooker and cook on high pressure for another 2 minutes. Repeat as needed. Using tongs, transfer the octopus from the pressure cooker to a cutting board, discarding the onion. Reserve ¾ cup of the braising liquid.

Meanwhile, in a medium skillet over medium heat, add the olive oil, garlic, bell pepper, and jalapeños. When the mixture comes to a simmer, turn down the heat to low and continue to cook until the garlic is soft, about 12 minutes. Reserve.

When the octopus is cool enough to touch, use a sharp knife to cut the head off above the eyes (where the head narrows). Moving down 1½ inches, make another horizontal cut across the body below the eyes. Discard the section with the eyes, but keep the rest.

To remove the beak, flip the leg portion over to see the underside, and locate a small, hard black dot (the beak) in the center of the body. Make a deep incision from the beak toward a section where two legs meet, then open the flaps to reveal the whole beak. Using a paring knife, gently cut the beak from the body. Remove it and discard. Use the knife to separate the eight legs. Cut the head into ½-inch strips. Cut the legs into 5-inch pieces, discarding the skinniest end bits. Arrange the sliced octopus in a single layer in a 9 by 13-inch baking pan. Add the reserved ¾ cup of the braising liquid to the garlic-oil mixture and pour over the octopus. Place the pan in the oven and cook until the peppers and garlic skins begin to brown, 20 minutes. Remove from the oven, season to taste with salt, and serve immediately with the potatoes and bread.

Cocimiento

(A Mountain and Ocean Stew)

Serves 4 to 6

Olive oil for sautéing

1 pound Portuguese sausage (linguiça), chopped

1 yellow onion, chopped

3 jalapeño chiles or Thai chiles, chopped

3 ribs celery, chopped

3 carrots, chopped

4 garlic cloves, chopped

1 bunch cilantro, stems and leaves chopped separately

One 750 ml bottle dry white wine (the cheap kind)

4 cups water

Flaky sea salt

One 1- to 2-pound whole lobster

3 red potatoes, chopped

½ pound boneless, skinless yellowtail fillet, cut into 1-inch pieces

⅓ pound Manila clams or mussels

Juice of 2 lemons

Freshly ground black pepper

On a dive trip to Robinson Crusoe Island in Chile, I became friends with the staff of the seaside lodge I was staying at. The waitresses asked to join me for a dive on their day off. They wanted to dive for pulpo (octopus). We had immediate success and found some right away in the shallows. We swam out to deeper water to gut the pulpo and were instantly swarmed by a school of huge vidriola (yellowtail)! I speared two and the girls helped me wrestle them in. We were all so elated returning to shore. The chef marveled when we gave her our catches. That night she served us the most decadent stew called cocimiento. She added our fish and octopus to a rich broth filled with shellfish, lobster, sausage, and veggies.

This cherished meal of Chile originates back to when mountain people and ocean people would come together to share their harvests in the same pot. The ingredients vary depending on location and what people have on hand, but it's always a harmony of seafood, meat, vegetables, and lots of wine!

In a large Dutch oven or saucepot, add enough olive oil to coat the bottom of the pot and warm the oil over medium-high heat. Add the chorizo, onion, and chiles, and stir. When the onions have softened, about 2 minutes, add the celery, stir, and continue to cook for 1 more minute, then stir in the carrots. After 5 minutes, add the garlic and the cilantro stems, and cook for 1 minute. Add the wine, water, and two pinches of salt, bring to a boil, then lower the heat to medium-low and bring to a simmer.

Put the whole lobster in the broth and cook for 7 minutes, then transfer it to a cutting board. Let the broth simmer. Once the lobster is cool enough to touch, twist the tail off. Use the heel of a knife to crack the tail shell and cut into the underside to help break the shell apart. Pull out the lobster meat, slice it, and reserve. Put the tail shell and legs back in the broth. (The shells do not need to be removed before serving, but should not be eaten.) Cover, and let simmer for 30 minutes.

Add the potatoes and stir. Cover again and cook for another 15 minutes.

Season the fish with salt. Add the clams, lobster tail meat, and fish to the broth, and cover and cook until the clams have opened and the fish has cooked through, about 5 minutes. Add the lemon juice and cilantro leaves and stir. Taste and adjust the seasoning with salt and pepper. Ladle the soup into bowls, making sure to get pieces of everything in each portion.

Fish Alternatives

Trevally
Snapper
Sea bass

BREWING

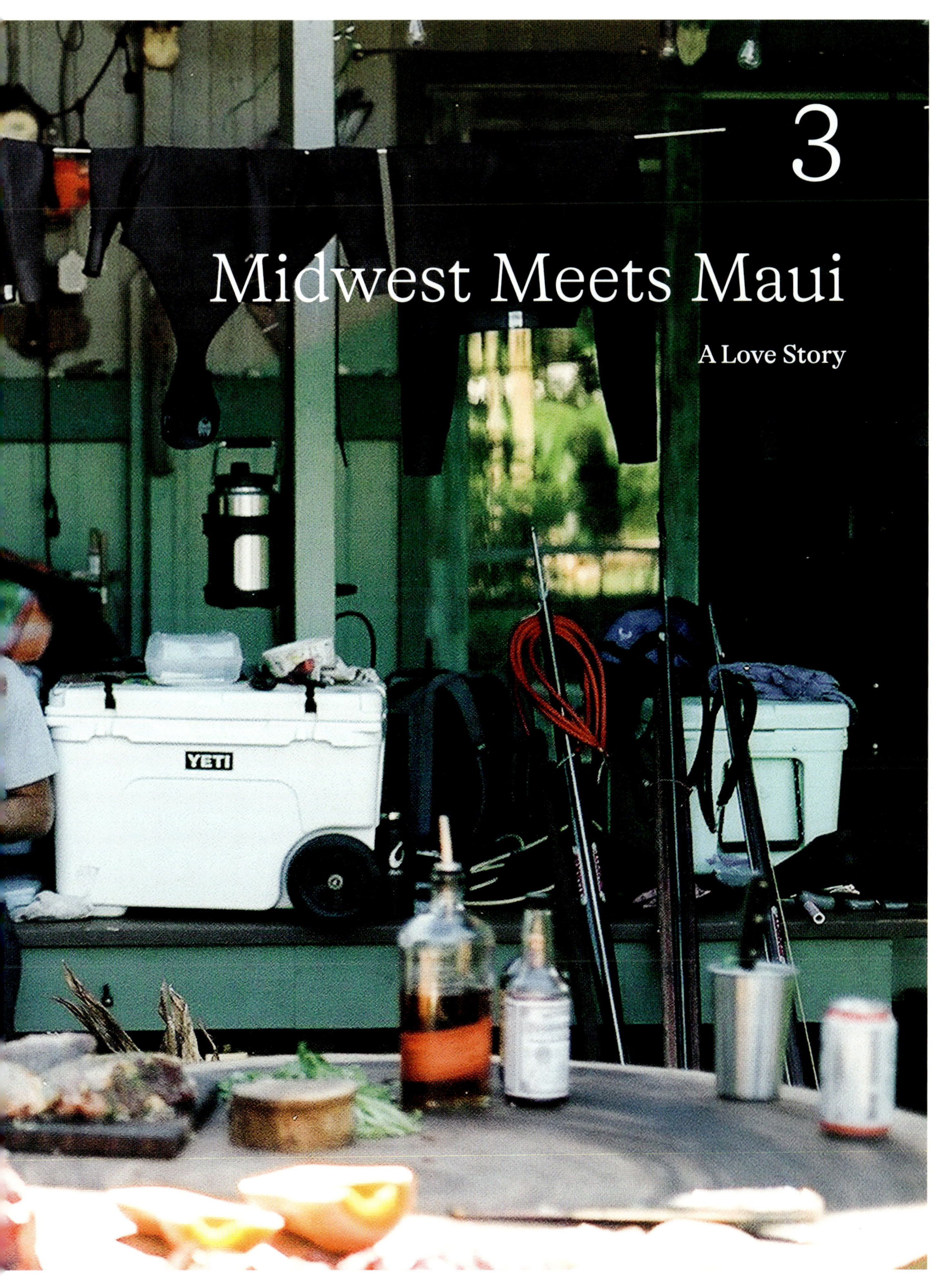

3

Midwest Meets Maui

A Love Story

I remember the night I fell for Justin. It was on our "four-day first date" in Maui. We had met on the set of a TV show. He was on the production side and I was spearfishing and cooking in front of the camera. I had a crush on him the whole time. His hotel room was across from mine, and we awkwardly avoided eye contact while saying good-morning and did our best to act normal and professional, so it wasn't until after our shoot wrapped that we allowed the sparks to fly. Without a TV show to bring us together, the only way to see about our connection was to make a major move. And that he did. He flew all the way to Maui from Minnesota for our first date and I came by boat from Moloka'i after a week of diving with friends. I felt insecure about being so weathered, dirty, and salty but happy to have a cooler full of freshly harvested fish and lobster. I was so nervous and excited, and we were both way too polite and awkward. We stayed in a small cabin in Hana, Maui. Soon the awkwardness was replaced with genuine fun. I took him diving and cooked so many meals straight from my heart. Meals that came from my family and roots.

One evening, Justin and I were outside cleaning some fish I had caught and planned to steam whole. I worried that it would be weird for him to have our meal staring back at him, but I showed him how I scale and gut fish and he jumped right in to help. I grabbed a nice cleaned goatfish and took it inside to prepare for dinner. It started raining hard. I looked outside, expecting to see Justin running for shelter, but he sat there in the grass getting poured on, scaling fish after fish and practicing everything I showed him. My heart felt something as I stood there, in awe of this man in the rain. I can still see and feel it all so clearly today.

Later that night, the sky cleared, and we ate our fish under the stars. My insecurities of how he'd feel about the meal melted away because Justin picked the fish clean to the bone with his bare hands and exclaimed to the sky with such enthusiasm how damn good it was. I could not believe how perfect a moment I was living in nor would I know that we would marry in that exact spot years later. On the last day of his trip, we went to visit my parents and sister in upcountry Maui. My mom made us so many meals in our short time together, and as soon as Justin was out of the room, she looked at me, eyes wide with amazement, and said, "Kim, he's such a good eater!" I nodded immediately. "Right, Mom?! I can't even believe what a good eater he is!" My sister laughed at both of us and said, "You weirdos sound like you're talking about a baby!"

Justin has embraced the food of my heart with such appreciation and gratitude. He is absolutely my favorite person to cook for. His wholehearted integration into this place I call home means the world to me, and I feel with utter importance the need to return the honor. Justin grew up on wild game meat, potatoes, and lots of vegetables. He learned to hunt white-tailed deer from his dad and his mom grew up on a farm that his uncle still runs today. Justin has taken on the qualities of both his parents, becoming fascinated with bowhunting and becoming such a dedicated gardener. He has turned our whole little property into a food-providing oasis. I feel so grateful to always have collard greens and spinach on hand as well as fresh herbs and a variety of fruit from the trees in our backyard.

Less than a year after our four-day first date, Justin gave up his main career as a snowboarding cinematographer to start a life with me here in Hawai'i. We didn't have much money at the time, but we had big dreams. I taught him how to freedive and he took to it so well. He's not only become my dive partner but also one of the most capable and talented underwater cinematographers in the world. It makes me so happy that we took a chance with love and let our own talents and passions combine to show us the way. Our life is a pure fusion of our different roots, and these recipes are exactly that. They are all a part of our journey together and honor where we came from.

Cured and Smoked Fish and Venison

Makes 6 ounces of fish or venison

Fish

1 tablespoon granulated sugar

1 tablespoon fine sea salt

½-pound boneless, skinless 'ahi (yellowfin tuna) fillet or any medium to large fish (you want a solid slab)

2 tablespoons coarsely ground black pepper

Zest of 1 lemon

Venison

½ pound venison from the hindquarter, such as the top round, eye of round, or sirloin, 1 to 2 inches thick

1 tablespoon granulated sugar

1 tablespoon fine sea salt

2 tablespoons coarsely ground black pepper

When Justin and I first got together, I'd bring home the fish and he'd bring home the meat. As I write this, I'm marinating a piece of red stag (deer I bowhunted in New Zealand) and Justin just got home from diving with a cooler full of fish. I love that we have both learned from each other and that with all the great food coming through our door we try our best to preserve what we can. We love smoking cured meat and fish to give them extra flavor and to make them last longer, and they're so nice to always keep in our fridge to use for quick snacks, charcuterie, or sandwiches. Curing is a simple procedure; all you really need is salt, sugar, and time.

To make the fish: In a small bowl, combine the sugar and salt and stir. Rub the sugar-salt mixture over the fish until it is thoroughly coated. Place the fish in a resealable plastic bag and refrigerate 8 hours or overnight with a light weight (like a plate) on top of it.

The next day, remove the fish from the accumulated brine. Rinse it briskly and pat it dry. In a small bowl, combine the pepper and lemon zest, and rub it together with your fingers to release the oil in the lemon skin. Coat the cured fillet evenly with the pepper-lemon mixture.

To smoke the fish, preheat a smoker to 165°F. Place the fish on the grate and close the smoker. Smoke for 1 to 3 hours (it will be lightly smoked in 1 hour, while 3 hours yields firmer, more assertively smoked fish). Transfer the fish to a plate and let it cool. Serve immediately, sliced thinly, or store in the fridge for up to 1 week wrapped in a paper towel in an airtight container.

To make the venison: Two days before you plan to serve the venison, start preparing the meat. Trim the white membrane from the venison and discard. In a small bowl, combine the sugar and salt and stir. Rub the sugar-salt mixture over the meat until it is thoroughly coated. Place the venison in a resealable plastic bag and refrigerate for 48 hours with a small weight (like a plate) on top of it.

Remove the venison from the accumulated brine, lightly rinse off the sugar-salt cure, and pat it dry. Coat the cured venison evenly with black pepper. Preheat a smoker to 165°F. Place the venison on the grate and smoke for 3 hours. Raise the smoker's heat to 400°F and smoke the venison for 15 minutes. Transfer the venison to a plate and let it cool.

To serve, slice the venison thinly. The smoked venison will keep in the fridge, covered, for up to 1 week, or you can freeze it for later use.

Fish Alternatives

Marlin
Snapper
Trevally

Cured Venison Reuben

Serves 2

⅓ cup chopped dill pickles

⅓ cup mayonnaise

4 teaspoons ketchup

1 tablespoon stone-ground mustard

2 teaspoons Worcestershire sauce

1 teaspoon freshly squeezed lemon juice

4 slices sourdough bread

Slices of sharp white Cheddar cheese

Sliced pickled jalapeño chiles (optional)

4 ounces Cured and Smoked Venison (page 97) or pastrami, sliced thinly

½ cup sauerkraut, squeezed and drained

Butter for sautéing

In addition to curing and smoking venison, Justin also loves making batches of sauerkraut and baking homemade sourdough bread. So I got excited when a little lightbulb flashed in my head and I got the idea to combine these three creations into a Reuben-like sandwich. As I write this chapter, it becomes ever clear to me that I love watching Justin light up over food. He's such an enthusiastic eater and, sure enough, this sandwich got the full ecstatic reaction out of him and gave me the dopamine hit I love from making him happy.

In a small bowl, combine the pickles, mayonnaise, ketchup, mustard, Worcestershire sauce, and lemon juice, and stir to combine. Spread the pickle mixture on one side of each bread slice. Top one of the bread slices with enough slices of cheese to cover the bread, half of the jalapeños (if using), half of the venison, half of the sauerkraut, and the other slice of bread (with the pickle mixture facing inward). Repeat to make the other sandwich.

In a pan large enough to fit both sandwiches, melt a pat of butter over medium-high heat, then add the sandwiches to the pan. Turn down the heat to low. If you have a grill press, place it on top of the sandwiches (or you can use another pan as a weight instead). Cook until the bottoms of the sandwiches turn golden brown, about 10 minutes, then flip, adding another piece of butter to the pan. Cook the other side until golden, then transfer the sandwiches to a plate. Cut and serve immediately.

Fish Tacos with Cilantro Lime-Jalapeño Aioli

Serves 4 (8 to 10 tacos)

Fish

1½ pounds any boneless, skinless fish that can be cut into ¾-inch cubes (I prefer mahimahi)

2 tablespoons taco spice or a mix of cumin and chili powder or your preferred spice blend

Olive oil for sautéing

1 bunch cilantro stems, chopped

3 garlic cloves, minced

½ lime

For Serving

Olive oil

8 to 10 six-inch corn or flour tortillas

One 15-ounce can black beans, rinsed and drained

2 cups thinly sliced greens of your choice (arugula, lettuce, spinach, or cabbage work well)

1 cup grated white sharp Cheddar cheese

Cilantro Lime-Jalapeño Aioli (recipe follows)

1 large avocado, sliced

1 large tomato, diced

½ cup diced red onion

Chopped fresh cilantro

Lime wedges

Street Mango Salsa (recipe follows)

Justin has become my favorite spearfishing partner, and that's a pretty special thing to say because it wasn't always the case. Even though I have always enjoyed my time in the water with him, I also craved time with my regular dive partners to push myself. It's fun to dive with people so good that you need to bring your A game every time. But Justin kept coming along, whether to film us or shoot fish, and soon he started to push himself too. He started filming us at depths he couldn't reach before. He started understanding fish behavior and the tiny nuances of hunting strategies. One day, my friend and dive partner Mark Healey floated at the surface, watching Justin hunt fish seventy-five feet down with smooth perfection. Mark poked his head up and asked the exact words going through my mind: "When did Justin get so fucking good?"

Spearfishing with my husband is currently at the very top of my list of my favorite things to do. And after long, wonderful days spent underwater, our favorite way to celebrate is with cold beer and fish tacos. I know it's a big claim, but my fish tacos are the absolute best (like, in the world). It's all in the cilantro lime-jalapeño aioli and the way it makes our taste buds scream when it's slathered over fish and hugged in a good-quality tortilla.

To cook the fish: With a sharp knife, cut the fish into ¾-inch cubes. Season the fish generously with the taco spice mix, then toss with your hands to evenly coat the cubes. In a large skillet (a well-seasoned cast-iron one is best) over medium-high heat, add enough olive oil to coat the bottom of the skillet, and warm the oil. When the oil shimmers (about 1 minute), add the fish to the skillet in a single, even layer. Let the fish brown on one side for 3 minutes before flipping; I prefer a spatula over tongs to do this. You want to create beautiful brown edges on all sides of the fish chunks, stirring only when needed (stirring less will also help keep the fish intact). After the second side is brown, an additional 3 minutes, add the cilantro stems and garlic and stir. After 1 minute, squeeze the lime half directly into the pan. Immediately turn off the heat.

Fish Alternatives

Halibut
Hogfish
Grouper

continued

Fish Tacos with Cilantro Lime-Jalapeño Aioli

continued

To warm the tortillas: In a large skillet over medium-high heat, add enough olive oil to coat the bottom of the skillet. Add a tortilla and heat on one side until it begins to brown, about 1 minute, then flip to heat the other side. You may need to add more oil as you brown each tortilla. Store the heated tortillas in a tortilla warmer if you have one, or stack them on a plate and cover with a kitchen towel.

To assemble the tacos: On a warmed tortilla, add the fish, beans, greens, and cheese. Slather the assembled tacos with the aioli. Garnish with avocado, tomato, red onion, and cilantro. Serve immediately with the lime wedges and mango salsa.

Cilantro Lime-Jalapeño Aioli

Makes about 2 cups

1 cup mayonnaise

1 cup coarsely chopped fresh cilantro leaves

½ cup jarred jalapeño chiles, diced small (see Note)

3 tablespoons sour cream

Zest and juice of 2 large limes

1 teaspoon orange zest (optional)

1 tablespoon freshly squeezed orange juice (optional)

Note: *The jalapeños have to be jarred! I love the vinegary flavor that comes from jarred jalapeños over fresh ones for this recipe.*

This aioli can be made up to 1 week in advance and stored covered in the fridge. When making this for the tacos, there will most likely be plenty of aioli left over, which is great in sandwiches, wraps, or dolloped into soups.

In a medium bowl, combine the mayonnaise, cilantro, jalapeños, sour cream, lime zest and juice, and orange zest and juice (if using), and stir. Scoop into a small serving bowl, cover, and chill in the fridge.

Street Mango Salsa

Yields 2½ cups

2 large ripe mangoes, diced into ⅓-inch cubes

⅔ cup fresh cilantro, roughly chopped

½ large red onion, diced small

1 garlic clove, finely grated

1 teaspoon flaky sea salt

Hot sauce to taste

Juice of 2 limes

Our neighbors Vern and Ginny have a huge mango tree in their yard that hangs over the fence and drops mangoes by the dozens onto the road. Buddy and Justin always pick up and salvage any road mangoes that aren't too severely bruised from their falls. Granted, Vern and Ginny would let Buddy pick any prime mango he wants, but he and Justin simply enjoy their little Easter egg hunt of searching for them on the street. Most of the time, I have to cut away the bruised parts of the street mangoes, and my go-to recipe for using the remaining good pieces is mango salsa. It's great with chips or topped on seared fish.

In a medium bowl, add the mangoes, cilantro, onion, garlic, salt, hot sauce, and lime juice, and stir to combine. Taste and adjust the seasoning. The salsa will keep covered in the fridge for 3 days.

Hunter's Loco Moco

Serves 4

1 pound ground elk, venison, or lean beef

Flaky sea salt and freshly ground black pepper

Olive oil for sautéing

½ large yellow onion, cut into ¼-inch slices

2 garlic cloves, roughly minced

7 tablespoons salted butter

6 ounces king oyster or button mushrooms, sliced

3 tablespoons all-purpose flour

3 cups water

2 tablespoons Better Than Bouillon Roasted Beef or Chicken Base

1 tablespoon shoyu

4 cups cooked white rice

4 eggs

Chopped green onion, white and green parts, for garnishing

Chili Pepper Water (page 34) for garnishing (optional)

Loco moco, a soul food of Hawai'i, consists of a burger over white rice, smothered in brown gravy, and topped with a sunny-side-up egg. There is nothing light about it, but damn, it sure is tasty! When Justin first moved to Hawai'i, he brought some ground elk with him, which I used to make him his first loco moco. He instantly declared that it was his new favorite food!

Using your hands, divide the elk into four patties that are roughly ½ inch high. Generously season both sides of the patties with salt and pepper, making sure every bite of the patty contains flakes of salt and pepper.

In a large skillet over medium-high heat, warm 2 tablespoons of olive oil. When the oil gets hot and begins to shimmer, about 90 seconds, place the patties in the skillet with enough room so that they are not touching each other. (You will most likely need to do this in two batches.) Gently press the patties with a spatula.

After 1 minute, turn down the heat to medium or medium-low. (This will give the patty an initial sear but ensures that it cooks through without burning.) Cook for about 3 minutes and flip the patties. Raise the heat to medium or medium-high and repeat the process on the other side. If the skillet gets too dry while cooking, add a bit more oil. (The goal here is to get a burger patty with a deep brown crust that's cooked all the way through. I'm a firm believer in medium to well-done burgers.) When both sides are nicely browned, remove the patties from the skillet.

Without wiping the skillet, add 1 tablespoon of olive oil and keep the temperature at medium-high heat. Add the onion and cook for about 3 minutes, stirring occasionally with a wooden spoon or spatula and scraping any brown bits off the bottom of the skillet. Lightly salt the onion. Add half of the garlic to the skillet, stir, and cook for 1 minute. Transfer the onion-garlic mixture to a small bowl and return the skillet to the stove.

While the skillet is hot, add 2 tablespoons of the butter, continuing to cook at medium-high heat. Once the butter is melted, add the mushrooms and spread them evenly in a single layer so that every piece touches the skillet. Lightly season with salt and drizzle olive oil over the mushrooms while they begin to cook. Let the mushrooms cook on one side to get a browned sear, roughly 2 minutes, then flip and stir them. Add the remaining garlic to the skillet. Stir and cook for 1 minute. Transfer the mushroom mixture into a bowl or plate and reserve.

continued

Hunter's Loco Moco

continued

While the pan is still hot, add 3 tablespoons of butter, continuing to cook at medium-high heat. When the butter melts, use a wooden spoon to scrape the bottom of the pan to get all of those delicious brown bits mixed in. Add the flour to the melted butter and stir to thoroughly incorporate both ingredients. As the flour and butter darken, stir continuously for about 2 minutes. The mixture should start to develop a nutty aroma and color.

Swap the wooden spoon for a whisk. Slowly add 2 cups of the water in a steady stream while whisking. When the water has been smoothly incorporated, go back to the wooden spoon to keep mixing, and bring the gravy to a rapid simmer. Let it thicken but keep stirring continuously so it doesn't burn. After 3 minutes, add the remaining 1 cup of water and thoroughly scrape the sides and bottom of the pan with the spoon so nothing burns. Add the bouillon base to the gravy and stir. Then add the shoyu, season with pepper, stir, and bring to a boil. Turn down the heat to low and let simmer until the gravy coats the back of the spoon, 7 to 10 minutes. Remove from the heat.

To serve: Scoop a heaping mound of rice on a plate, then pour a ladle of the gravy over the rice. Top with a burger patty, some of the onion-garlic mixture, and mushrooms. Smother it in more gravy.

Once the plate is assembled, heat a large pan over high heat and melt the remaining 2 tablespoons of butter. Once the butter is melted and bubbly, crack an egg right into the pan. Lightly season with salt and pepper. When the egg white is set and the yolk is still runny, 1 minute, turn down the heat to low and cook for an additional 2 minutes. (If you want an over-easy egg, flip your egg after 1 minute and continue to cook for 30 seconds.) Place the egg on top of the assembled dish. Repeat with the remaining ingredients. Garnish with the green onion and serve immediately with chili pepper water, if using.

Love the Whole Animal

To truly love someone is to love them wholly; to embrace all of them and lean in with care for their tougher parts. It's a celebration of everything that makes up a special being—not a conditional love that celebrates only the easy surface stuff and shies away from the rest. On the contrary, true love takes work, but only because it runs deeply. This is true with people and, most definitely, with food. So much of my life is spent leaning into the often unwanted parts of food, embracing the tougher cuts, or figuring out ways to preserve food so that it can last over time and not go to waste. It's a labor of love to my prey, to the planet, and to all living beings that make this world go round.

Marlin Cobb Salad

Serves 2

2 eggs

½ pound boneless, skinless marlin fillet or other firm white fish, cut into 1-inch cubes

Flaky sea salt and freshly ground black pepper

Avocado oil for sautéing

¼ pound Cured and Smoked Venison (page 97), finely chopped, or 6 strips cooked bacon, chopped

1 medium head green-leaf lettuce, washed and torn into bite-size pieces

1 ripe avocado, cut into 1-inch cubes

1 cup chopped grape tomatoes

4 ounces blue or feta cheese, crumbled

Dressing

½ cup sour cream, plus more as needed

¼ cup mayonnaise, plus more as needed

3 tablespoons whole milk, plus more as needed

Juice from ½ lemon

3 tablespoons finely chopped fresh flat-leaf parsley

3 tablespoons finely chopped chives

1 tablespoon dried dill

½ garlic clove, finely grated

Flaky sea salt and freshly ground black pepper

Fish Alternatives

Halibut
Ono (wahoo)
Tuna

I'm a bacon-and-eggs girl and Justin is a fruit-and-granola guy. He's always making me drink more water and eat more veggies, so, when I think of salad, I think of Justin. One day, when Justin and I were hungry and I opened the fridge to see a bunch of salad veggies and a slab of freshly gifted blue marlin from our fisherman neighbor, Chris, I made us a Cobb salad. And wow! It's the perfect way to use cooked marlin, which can sometimes be a bit tough and dry. I chopped it in cubes and sautéed it, and appreciated its firmness—just like chicken breast! And when smothered in blue cheese and ranch dressing with all the Cobb toppings, it sure hit the spot.

Prepare an ice bath by filling a medium bowl with cold water and ice cubes. Place the eggs in a small pot and add enough water to cover them. Cover the pot with a lid, then bring the water to a boil over medium-high heat. Turn off the heat and let the pot sit, covered, for 7 minutes. Using a slotted spoon, transfer the eggs to the ice bath. When the eggs are cool, peel them, then chop and reserve.

Meanwhile, season the marlin with salt and a generous amount of pepper. In a medium skillet over medium-high heat, add enough avocado oil to coat the bottom of the skillet, and heat the oil until it is searing hot. Working in batches, place the cubes of fish in a single layer in the skillet so they aren't touching. Cook until the fish develops a brown crust, flipping when necessary, about 4 minutes, then cook the other side until it browns, about 3 minutes. Transfer to a plate and reserve. Repeat with the remaining marlin, adding more oil if necessary.

Wipe the skillet clean (or grab a fresh one). Add enough oil to coat the bottom of the skillet and, continuing over medium-high heat, warm the oil. Add the venison and cook until it crisps up, stirring occasionally, about 5 minutes. Transfer to a plate and reserve.

To make the dressing: In a medium bowl, add the sour cream, mayonnaise, milk, lemon juice, parsley, chives, dill, and garlic. Season with salt and pepper and mix thoroughly. Taste and adjust the seasoning. If the dressing is too thick, add more milk, 1 tablespoon at a time. If it's too thin, add more mayo or sour cream, 1 tablespoon at a time. Reserve.

To assemble the salad: Divide the lettuce into two bowls. Season with salt and pepper, then top each bowl with half of the marlin, venison, avocado, tomatoes, and cheese. Serve with the dressing alongside or drizzled over the top.

Fish Tataki

(Seared Sashimi with Tangy Crispy Garlic Sauce)

Serves 4 to 6 as an appetizer

1 pound sashimi-grade aku (skipjack tuna) fillet

2 tablespoons avocado oil

3 tablespoons Cajun spice blend

Tangy Crispy Garlic Sauce

5 tablespoons shoyu

2 tablespoons freshly squeezed lemon or lime juice

2 teaspoons granulated or light brown sugar

2 tablespoons peeled, minced fresh ginger (roughly a 2-inch knob)

2 tablespoons chopped green onion, white and green parts

2 tablespoons minced fresh cilantro

3 tablespoons toasted sesame oil

4 garlic cloves, coarsely chopped

Fish Alternatives

'Ahi
Snapper
Ono (wahoo)

Tataki is elevated sashimi. It's worth taking the time to sear the edges of the raw fish and not just for the stunning looks of it, but because those cooked edges have a meatier bite. Those edges also soak up the sauce, which is punchy with strong notes of citrus and should be spooned onto each piece with love. But the real game changer, my friends, is the crispy brown garlic. It takes umami to another level when you take the time to brown your garlic. Browning garlic in sesame oil creates one of my favorite smells of all time. My signature touch on a tataki platter is to make a rose out of the final fish pieces as a centerpiece. It's quite simple to do, but it adds a special touch and it's my favorite way to give Justin flowers.

With a sharp knife, trim the bloodlines from the aku fillet (see page 247). Cut the cleaned fillet into long rectangular pieces roughly 2 inches wide and 1 to 1½ inches tall (any length will work, as you will eventually thinly slice the fillet).

Set a plate near the stove. In a large skillet over high heat, heat the avocado oil. While you wait for the oil to get hot, generously coat all the long sides of the fish with the Cajun spice blend. Working with one piece at a time, place a block of the spice-coated fish in the hot oil, and press it with a spatula for roughly 5 seconds. (This is a super-fast, high-heat situation—not the time to be a hero. Make it easy on yourself by doing only one piece at a time.) Repeat on each side. The outside should be cooked and the inside raw. Don't overcook—seriously, 5 seconds on each side will be good if your pan is hot enough. Immediately place the seared block on the plate and cool it down in the freezer, uncovered, for about 10 minutes.

To make the sauce: While the fish is cooling in the freezer, make the sauce by combining the shoyu, lemon juice, and sugar in a medium bowl. Stir with a spoon until the sugar dissolves. Add the ginger, green onion, and cilantro to the sauce, then stir to combine, and reserve.

In a small skillet over medium to high heat, heat the sesame oil. When the oil begins to shimmer, add the garlic, stirring constantly to avoid burning. Cook the garlic until it is crispy and golden to medium brown in color, 2 to 3 minutes. Once the majority of the garlic has turned golden, turn

continued

patagonia

Fish Tataki

continued

off the heat. The hot oil will continue to cook the rest of the garlic more gently without burning the browned pieces. Let it cool for 1 minute. Add the crispy garlic and sesame oil to the shoyu sauce and stir to combine.

Take the cooked fish out of the freezer. Slice the blocks width-wise into ¼-inch slices. For this process, it helps to have a really sharp knife so that the fish stays intact.

To serve: Choose a platter that has a 1-inch lip to hold the sauce. Fan out and lightly overlap the fish slices on the platter so that the majority of the fish's surface is exposed. (I like to choose a circular platter and arrange the fish in concentric circles. For the center, I make a rose shape out of the cut fish by arranging four or five slices in a row with a slight overlap. Then, moving width-wise, I tightly roll the pieces together, so that when placed upright, the slices form the petals of a rose. I place the roll in the center of the platter, then let the top edges of the pieces unfurl into a flower shape.) Spoon the sauce onto the fish (make sure each piece gets its share of the garlic, cilantro, and sauce) and then drizzle the remainder on top. Serve immediately.

Grilled Rosemary Mustard Chops

Serves 4 to 6

½ cup olive oil
½ cup Dijon mustard
½ cup fresh rosemary leaves
7 garlic cloves, peeled
3 pounds venison, lamb rib, or loin chops (see Note)
Flaky sea salt and freshly ground black pepper

Over the years, Justin and I have enjoyed this meal as our classic date-night-at-home dinner so much that we made it for all the guests at our wedding. I've always been a fan of this marinade for grilled lamb chops, and as we slowly switched from store-bought meat to the wild game we harvested ourselves, I wondered, why not venison? My hunting friend Sean, along with Justin, made my dreams come true one day when they figured out how to saw through the rib bones to bring home bone-in racks of venison straight from the field. At first, I'd marinate and cook the rack whole, but I later realized they were even tastier when cut into individual chops, then marinated. The marinade's flavor covers more surface area this way, and the grilling becomes so fast and easy. We call them venison lollipops. I'll never forget the day before our wedding; Sean dropped off a huge cooler full of venison racks he had been saving for us, and Justin and I stood in my parents' kitchen for hours, hand-cutting every lollipop ourselves. I remember just smiling while we worked until we both broke out in laughter, asking ourselves, "Who does this right before they get married?" But it's in those moments when I realize how much I love this man, and our lollipops were such a hit the next day!

The day before you plan to serve, prep the marinade for the venison. In a blender, add the olive oil, mustard, rosemary, and garlic, and blend on high speed until smooth, about 2 minutes.

Season the venison with salt and pepper. Generously coat all the parts of the venison with the rosemary-mustard mixture. Place the coated venison in a large nonreactive container, cover, and place in the fridge overnight.

The next day when you're ready to cook, preheat a grill to 400°F. When the grill is hot, place the chops on the grill and cook until browned, 2 to 3 minutes, then flip and repeat on the other side. Transfer the chops to a serving platter, let them rest for 1 to 2 minutes, and serve immediately.

Note: *Because I get my venison from hunting, to make this, I usually start with a rib rack and separate each individual chop by cutting in between each rib bone. Some people like to clean the rib bones "French" style by scraping all the meat and fat off one end of the bone to create a handle, but I don't do this because I think leaving them on makes it more delicious.*

Collard Greens with Shoyu and Butter

Serves 4 to 6

3 tablespoons salted butter

1 pound collard greens, destemmed and roughly chopped

3 garlic cloves, minced

2 tablespoons shoyu

Our friend Jen gave us a cutting from her amazingly healthy bushel of collard greens and, with Justin's loving care, it basically grew into a palm tree in our yard. People can't help but gawk when they stop to ask what kind of plant it is. And we have had an abundance of collard greens ever since. This recipe is such a winner; the simple, fast process of heating butter, garlic, and greens and finishing with shoyu elevates any leafy cooking green into a true masterpiece. This technique is great with bok choy and choy sum too!

In a large skillet over medium-high heat, melt the butter. When the butter is bubbling, add the collard greens. After 1 minute, use a spatula, tongs, or cooking chopsticks to gently turn over the greens so that the leaves on the bottom move to the top, and continue to cook. When the greens are wilted, about 2 minutes, sprinkle with the garlic, stir, and cook for 2 to 3 more minutes. Add the shoyu, stir, and turn off the heat. Serve immediately.

Osso Buco with Creamy Polenta

Serves 4 to 6

2 venison or beef shanks, sawed into six 2-inch thick pieces (about 2½ pounds total)

Flaky sea salt and freshly ground pepper

½ cup all-purpose flour

Olive oil for sautéing

1 yellow onion, finely chopped

4 ribs celery, finely chopped

2 carrots, scrubbed and finely chopped

3 garlic cloves, finely chopped

One 15-ounce can tomato sauce

One 14.5-ounce can diced tomatoes

2 cups water

1 cup dry red wine (I prefer Cabernet)

2 tablespoons Better Than Bouillon Roasted Chicken Base

1 tablespoon finely chopped fresh rosemary

1 tablespoon finely chopped fresh thyme

2 teaspoons dried oregano

3 dried bay leaves

Chopped fresh flat-leaf parsley for garnishing

Polenta

4 cups water, plus more for thinning

1 tablespoon Better Than Bouillon Roasted Chicken Base

1 cup dried yellow corn polenta

⅓ cup heavy cream

⅓ cup grated Parmigiano-Reggiano cheese

Flaky sea salt and freshly ground black pepper

When Justin and I bowhunt, we always keep the shanks—the calves of the animal. In comparison to other cuts, shank meat is quite tough. So sadly, the shanks are often left in the field by many hunters. Most people who use the meat end up throwing it into the grinder. Which is good but it's not osso buco good! Osso buco is an Italian delicacy of crosscut veal shanks, braised until super tender. The crosscut bones allow the eater to suck the marrow right out, and it is just heavenly. Venison and sheep are also great for osso buco. At home, we use a reciprocating saw to make our crosscuts, but you can get them done by a butcher.

Season the shanks with salt and pepper. Cover a large plate with the flour and dredge each shank. In a wide braising pan or Dutch oven over medium-high heat, add enough olive oil to coat the bottom of the pan, and warm the oil. Add the shanks and sear each side to a rich medium brown, about 12 minutes. Transfer to a plate and reserve.

Add another glug of olive oil to the pan, warm it, then add the onion and cook, scraping the bottom of the pan with a wooden spoon to mix in any bits of drippings. When the onion is soft, about 2 minutes, stir in the celery and carrots and cook until the vegetables begin to brown on the edges, 2 minutes, then stir in the garlic and cook for 1 additional minute. Add the tomato sauce, diced tomatoes, water, wine, bouillon base, rosemary, thyme, oregano, and bay leaves, and stir, scraping any brown bits off the bottom of the pan. Season with salt and pepper. Return the shanks to the pan and submerge them in the liquid. Turn down the heat to low, cover, and cook for 1 hour. Use tongs to flip the shanks over. Gently scrape the bottom of the pan to incorporate the browned bits and cook for 1 additional hour, checking occasionally to make sure nothing is scorching. Check to see if the meat is tender and falling off the bone by poking the shanks with a chopstick or a fork. If so, remove from the heat. If not, continue cooking for an additional 30 minutes, adding more water as needed. Taste and adjust the seasoning.

To make the polenta: In a medium pot over medium-high heat, mix the water and the bouillon base and bring to a boil. Turn down the heat to low, then gradually add the polenta while whisking. Continue to cook for 30 minutes, whisking for 1 minute every 5 minutes. If the polenta gets too thick, add more water ½ cup at a time. Turn off the heat and stir in the heavy cream and Parmigiano-Reggiano cheese. Season with salt and pepper.

To serve: Spoon the polenta onto a plate or bowl, top with a venison shank or two and a ladle of the sauce, sprinkle with parsley, and serve.

ʻUlu Tot Hotdish

(A Hawaiʻi-Style Version of a Midwestern Classic)

Serves 4 to 6

2½ pounds fresh spinach, or 20 ounces frozen, chopped spinach, defrosted and squeezed dry

Olive oil for sautéing

1 pound ground venison or lean beef

Flaky sea salt and freshly ground black pepper

½ yellow onion, finely chopped

8 ounces button mushrooms, sliced

1 garlic clove, minced

One 10½-ounce can cream of mushroom soup

8 ounces canned water chestnuts, drained and chopped

3½ cups grated sharp Cheddar cheese

1 recipe ʻUlu Tots (recipe follows), or 4 dozen store-bought frozen Tater Tots prepared to package directions

Chopped fresh chives for garnishing

continued

It turns out the people of Minnesota are really into casseroles. I once asked Justin what his favorite comfort food of his childhood was, and he replied proudly, "Tater Tot hotdish," which is Minnesotan for a casserole of meat and cheese topped with Tater Tots. I'd never seen or heard of a Tater Tot hotdish here in Hawaiʻi, so I thought it would be really special to recreate one for Justin. Inspired by a beef and frozen spinach casserole my mom used to make, I created one with ground venison and fresh spinach from the garden. For the tots, I wanted them to be homemade and started wondering if I could use the ever-abundant ʻulu (breadfruit) that grows like crazy in Hawaiʻi. It's a food that could feed the world if more people knew how to cook with it, and I've been slowly making it my mission to do exactly that. So, when my ʻulu tots came out great, that alone felt like a huge success to have another delicious ʻulu recipe under my belt. But the true prize was watching Justin's eyes widen with excitement when he saw his hometown pride hit our dinner table. As he ate it, he drifted away to somewhere cozy and happy, exclaiming praise with every bite.

To prepare the spinach (if using fresh): Add the spinach and 1 inch of water to a large pot and cover. Over medium-high heat, bring the water to a boil and then turn down the heat to simmer. Use tongs or cooking chopsticks to turn the spinach over and cover to cook for another 1 to 2 minutes. Drain the spinach in a colander. When the spinach is cool enough to touch, squeeze out the remaining liquid with your hands. Roughly chop the spinach and reserve.

To make the casserole: Preheat the oven to 350°F.

In a large ovenproof skillet over medium-high heat, add enough olive oil to coat the bottom of the skillet, and warm the oil. Place the venison in the skillet and press it down with a spatula. Turn down the heat to medium. When the venison has browned, about 4 minutes, flip to repeat on the other side. Break apart the meat into small pieces. Season with salt and pepper. Add the onion, mushrooms, and garlic, and continue to cook, stirring occasionally. When the mushrooms are soft, about 6 minutes, add the cream of mushroom soup. Fill the can with water, scrape the remaining soup off the sides of the can, and add the water to the venison mixture. Add the water chestnuts, stir, and cook for 1 additional minute. Turn off the heat and slowly stir in 1½ cups of the cheese until it melts.

'Ulu Tot Hotdish

continued

Fold in the spinach. Taste and adjust the seasoning. Sprinkle the top with 1 cup of the cheese. Then place the skillet in the oven until the casserole is bubbling and the top has started to brown, about 20 minutes.

Take the skillet out of the oven, then arrange the 'ulu tots on top of the casserole and cover with the remaining 1 cup of cheese. Put the skillet back in the oven until the cheese has melted, about 10 minutes.

Let the casserole stand for 10 minutes, then garnish with the chives and serve.

'Ulu Tots

Makes 4 dozen

One 2-pound firm green 'ulu (breadfruit), quartered, or 9½ cups grated, parcooked 'ulu

Fine sea salt

1 tablespoon garlic powder

½ teaspoon freshly ground black pepper

¼ cup all-purpose flour

Olive oil for frying

Ketchup or dipping sauce of choice for serving

These tasty tots were created purely for the sake of trying to make a homemade version of Justin's hometown comfort food, the Tater Tot hotdish. But holy damn, I'm glad I did that because these tots are just so good on their own! My sister now proclaims them to be her favorite 'ulu recipe of all time. I love making a bunch and freezing them to fry later so that I can always have a quick and delicious side to go with a burger or a fun and easy snack for Buddy. For those of you who don't have access to 'ulu, I would not recommend substituting potatoes for this recipe. I have tried and it was a soggier, sadder version as potatoes require extra steps to get them crispy.

If starting with raw 'ulu, place a steamer basket in a large pot and add 1 inch of water. Add the 'ulu quarters and cover. Over medium-high heat, bring to a boil, then turn down the heat to medium-low and let simmer until a wooden chopstick can pierce through the thickest part, about 20 minutes. (Alternatively, use an electric pressure cooker. Place the 'ulu in the pressure cooker with 1 cup of water. Lock the lid into place and cook on high pressure for 8 minutes, then manually release the pressure. When the steam has released from the pressure cooker, remove the lid.) Transfer the 'ulu to a cutting board. When the cooked 'ulu is cool enough to touch, use a spoon to scrape the skin off. Remove all the parts of the core with a knife.

Do Ahead: *After the ʻulu tots are formed, they can be frozen for future use for up to 6 months. Place them in a single layer in a resealable plastic bag, then put them in the freezer. When you're ready to cook, proceed with the instructions starting with "Place a wire rack."*

Using the large holes of a box grater, grate the ʻulu. (You should have between 9½ and 10 grated cups.)

Place the grated ʻulu in a large bowl. Add 4 teaspoons of the salt, the garlic powder, and pepper, and toss with your hands. Add the flour and toss to coat again. The ʻulu should look somewhat loose, like uncooked oatmeal. (The mixture will look dry—don't be alarmed.) Using your hands, press and squeeze 3 tablespoons of the mixture together into oblong cylinders, like the shape of a Tater Tot. (If you're using frozen, parcooked ʻulu, you may need to squeeze a little harder.)

Place a wire rack over a baking pan and set near the stove. In a large skillet over medium-high heat, warm ½ inch of olive oil. When the oil is hot, about 3 minutes (test the heat by adding a tot and it will start to fry), work in batches to add the ʻulu tots in a single layer in the pan so they aren't touching. Cook until golden brown, turning frequently, about 10 minutes. Transfer the tots to the prepared wire rack to cool and season with salt. Repeat until all the tots have been cooked. Remove any stray bits from the oil and add more oil as necessary. Serve with ketchup or whatever dipping sauce you like.

4

Returning Home

Recipes of Hawaiʻi

Shortly after receiving my culinary degree, I worked at a very Americanized Mexican restaurant in the city of Honolulu. Cooking had once been a passion of mine, but this job fell very short of my hopes of fulfillment. Day after day, I worked long hours and cooked the same exact meals. The fish I worked with was frozen and imported from outside of Hawai'i, as was just about everything else on the menu. There was no story, no soul to the cooking. I was making food I had no connection to. I started to feel like a shell of person. That is, until that day when I went diving on my own and caught my own little fish. Humble little reef fish that I've never seen in a grocery store, let alone in a restaurant. But when seasoned simply and pan-fried to crispy perfection, they ended up being far superior to anything I had cooked in my culinary career. Why import so much when we have such rich biodiversity right here? Why copy the commercialized industry practices when we can honor our own ingredients through their own unique stories? The food of Hawaiʻi saved me and set me on a path, teaching me that what I was raised with deserves a seat at the table. Heck, it deserves to be the centerpiece.

These recipes are for Hawaiʻi and of Hawaiʻi. They come from the local community right here at home. You can find them in backyard barbecues, at graduation parties, or at babies' first birthdays (which by tradition is a huge celebration in Hawaiʻi). Although I've still tinkered and added my own twist to everything, the inspiration and roots of each recipe were born in these islands. Drying fish, wrapping laulau, frying he'e, and so many other practices in this chapter almost seem like a lost art, and it feels so important to cook this food and honor the humble, rootsy meals that raised me.

Kinilau

(Filipino-Style Poke)

Serves 4 to 6

1 medium goatfish, about 2 pounds, scaled and gutted

¾ cup shoyu

½ cup packed light brown sugar

Juice of ½ large lime or lemon

1 tablespoon white vinegar

1 tablespoon toasted sesame oil

¼ medium yellow onion, sliced thinly, then chopped into 2-inch pieces

3 green onions, white and green parts, chopped

1 tablespoon peeled, minced fresh ginger (a 1-inch knob)

2 Hawaiian chiles or chiles of your choice, minced

Kinilau was a dish taught to me by Garrett Tsutomu Lee—a fisherman, expert lure-maker, and one of my greatest teachers both in and out of the water. Whenever we would dive together, he would bring a mason jar of sweet, tangy shoyu vinegar sauce and keep it in a cooler on the boat while we spearfished. Whenever we shot a goatfish like a kūmū or munu, he would fillet and cube it with the skin on and add the fish to the cold jar of sauce. By the end of our dive day, we'd pop open a beer for the ride home and enjoy the firm, slightly chewy bites of marinated fish. We also did this with raw lobster. Although kinilau sounds like a Hawaiian word, I believe the origin is actually a Filipino dish called kinilaw. It's a ceviche of sorts made with raw fish and vinegar. One of the most intriguing things about food in Hawai'i is that so much of it is a fusion of different cultures because of the sugar plantation days. Chinese, Japanese, Filipino, and Portuguese immigrants were brought to Hawai'i to work in the sugar cane fields alongside Hawaiian plantation workers. It was hard work and a hard life, but people of different cultures sharing and eating together during their lunch breaks led to some of the most delightful adaptations of recipes. This recipe is a fusion of Hawaiian, Filipino, and Japanese flavors.

With a sharp knife, carve two boneless fillets off the whole fish (see page 245), keeping the skin on. Cut each fillet into 1-inch cubes and reserve.

In a medium bowl, mix the shoyu, sugar, lime juice, vinegar, sesame oil, yellow onion, green onions, ginger, and chiles. Taste and adjust the seasoning. Pour the sauce into a 1-quart jar with a lid. Add the fish, cover the jar, and shake gently to coat the fish pieces in the sauce. Place the jar in a cooler with ice, or refrigerate for at least 1 hour or up to 2 days. The fish will become firmer and sweet, almost candy-like, the longer you let it marinate. To serve, scoop the fish out of the sauce with a slotted spoon and place on a plate or eat with chopsticks straight from the jar.

Fish Alternatives

Rockfish
Raw shelled lobster
Enenue (sea chub)

Grilled Kala

(Unicornfish)

Serves 4 to 6

8 tablespoons salted butter
4 garlic cloves, coarsely chopped
Juice of ½ lemon
2 tablespoons shoyu, plus more for garnishing
One 2- to 3-pound whole kala (unicornfish), gutted (see Note)
Flaky sea salt and freshly ground black pepper
Chopped fresh flat-leaf parsley for garnishing (optional)

Kala is a unicornfish with thick leathery skin. The unique casing of this fish stands up to heat quite well, and when grilled whole over medium-low heat, all the natural oils of the fish get trapped, cooking the fish in a way that's perfectly moist and juicy. It also makes a simple, user-friendly contribution to any barbecue as you don't need aluminum foil—it comes with its own! Growing up, we would throw a kala on the grill and flip it over when one side was done. As the other side cooked, we'd peel back the skin of the finished side, and everyone would sit around the grill with their chopsticks, picking off succulent, moist bites of meat and dipping them into a communal bowl of shoyu, lemon, and chile. It makes my mouth water just writing that. My travels have since taken me to Tahiti, where kala is called ume and revered highly. The French influence on Tahiti led to dipping kala meat into sauces made of butter and garlic, and it tastes as decadent as lobster itself when treated that way. These days, I tend to do a fusion of the Hawaiian and Tahitian styles of the sauce, but the most important part of enjoying a grilled kala is to eat it with friends gathered around the grill while it's still hot.

Preheat a gas grill to 350°F, or prepare a wood or charcoal grill to medium-low heat (it is ready when you can hold your hand over the grate for 5 seconds).

Meanwhile, in a small saucepan over medium-high heat, melt the butter. When the butter is bubbly, add the garlic and stir. Continue to cook until the garlic is aromatic but not browned, about 2 minutes. Remove from the heat. Pour the butter-garlic mixture into a small bowl, add the lemon juice and shoyu, and stir.

When the grill is ready, place the fish directly on the hot grate. Cook until the skin is slightly charred and the juices are bubbling out of any cracks in the skin, about 20 minutes, then flip and repeat on the other side. To serve, use a chopstick or a knife to gently break the fish skin along the outer edges of the fish. Peel the skin back from the tail to the gill. Season the fish with salt and pepper, spoon the butter-garlic sauce over the fish, and garnish with shoyu and parsley, if using. Eat the fish straight off the bones with chopsticks. When one side has been picked clean, flip the fish over and repeat the process.

Note: *Kala should not be scaled and can be cooked whole directly over the fire. Acting as nature's tinfoil, its thick leathery skin seals the moisture and juices inside.*

YETI

Coconut Lime Octopus

Serves 4 to 6

One 2-pound octopus with the innards removed, previously frozen and defrosted (see Note)

Coarse sea salt and freshly ground black pepper

3 tablespoons salted butter

6 cups coarsely chopped, destemmed collard greens

3 garlic cloves, roughly chopped

One 13.5-ounce can unsweetened coconut milk

Juice of 2 limes

1 teaspoon granulated sugar (optional)

Chili Pepper Water (page 34)

Note: *If you have fresh octopus, gut it by pulling the head inside out and removing the innards. Freeze the octopus in a resealable bag or covered container for at least 4 days to tenderize it before defrosting.*

continued

This dish is a riff on a classic Hawai'i dish known as squid lū'au. I'm not sure why it was ever named squid lū'au when it was made with octopus, but either way, squid lū'au is a coconut milk stew of taro leaves and little bits of octopus, slow-cooked for hours until everything is a mush of tender goodness. It's delicious. I love squid lū'au, and this recipe with collard greens is a lighter, quicker, and tangier interpretation of it. Taro leaves must be cooked for at least an hour to remove the oxalate acid that can make your throat itch. Since I have a garden brimming with collard greens, I use them to make a quick sautéed version with octopus and coconut, which I love to finish with fresh lime.

Place the defrosted octopus in a large mixing bowl and sprinkle with 2 tablespoons of salt. Use your hands to vigorously squeeze, push, and press the entire octopus for 7 minutes—think of it as a deep tissue massage. At the thicker parts of the legs and head, apply pressure as you squeeze. Thoroughly rinse the octopus in cold running water. It will foam somewhat; keep rinsing until all the suds are gone and the water runs clear.

Place the cleaned octopus in the pot of an electric pressure cooker. Add 2 cups of water. Lock the lid into place and cook on high pressure for 12 minutes. Manually release the pressure. (Alternatively, cook the octopus on a stovetop: In a medium pot over medium-high heat, add the octopus and 3 cups of water. Bring to a boil, then turn down the heat to medium-low, cover, and let simmer for 1 hour.)

When the steam has released from the pressure cooker, remove the lid and pierce the thickest part of the octopus with a wooden chopstick or fork to make sure it punctures easily. If the octopus is not done, put it back in the pressure cooker and cook on high pressure for another 2 minutes. Repeat if necessary. Using tongs, transfer the octopus from the pressure cooker to a cutting board.

When the octopus is cool enough to touch, use a sharp knife to cut the head off above the eyes (where the head narrows). Moving down 1½ inches, make another horizontal cut across the body below the eyes. Discard the section with the eyes, but keep the rest.

To remove the beak, flip the leg portion over to see the underside, and locate a small, hard black dot (the beak) in the center of the body. Make a deep incision from the beak toward a section where two legs meet, then open the flaps to reveal the whole beak. Using a paring knife, gently cut

Coconut Lime Octopus

continued

the beak from the body. Remove it and discard. Use the knife to separate the eight legs. Cut the head and the legs into small bite-size pieces.

In a large pot over medium-high heat, melt the butter. Add the collard greens to the pot and stir. After the collard greens are wilted, about 2 minutes, add the garlic and stir. Cook for 1 more minute. Add the octopus pieces and coconut milk to the greens, and stir. Lightly season with salt and pepper. Add the lime juice and sugar (if using) and stir. Taste and adjust the seasoning. Serve immediately with chili pepper water.

Octopus

In Hawai'i, octopus is often referred to by its Japanese name, tako, or its Hawaiian name, he'e. These incredible creatures grow quickly (living no longer than eighteen months) and reproduce abundantly. And, with selective hunting methods like spearfishing and lure and line, the impact of harvesting on the ecosystem can be minimal. In places like Hawai'i, sourcing from small-scale, community-based fishers who follow traditional and sustainable harvesting practices helps ensure responsible fishing and supports local economies.

The main challenge that people encounter when preparing octopus is how the heck to get it tender. Some people beat it; some freeze it. I have even met people who have a spare washing machine dedicated for octopus tenderizing. Although it might sound like a crime to do this with fresh seafood, I am in the camp that if you catch an octopus and have time to freeze it, even if just for overnight, it greatly reduces the amount of massaging needed afterward. The invention of the Instant Pot has been a game changer for cooking octopus, and it still blows my mind that I can get a perfectly tender octopus in a little more than 10 minutes.

Shoyu Poke

Serves 2 as a main course or 4 as an appetizer

¼ cup shoyu

¼ cup thinly sliced yellow onion

2 tablespoons toasted sesame oil

1½ tablespoons granulated or light brown sugar

1 tablespoon minced, peeled ginger

2 Hawaiian chiles, minced, or your choice of fresh jalapeño chiles, Thai chiles, or red pepper flakes

¼ cup sliced green onions, white and green parts

1 pound fresh boneless, skinless ʻahi fillet, or any fish that you can eat raw (see page 20), cut into ½-inch cubes

Chopped avocado for garnishing (optional)

Chopped cucumber for garnishing (optional)

When people think of Hawaiʻi, they think of poke. And when they think of poke, they think about ruby-red cubes of ʻahi (yellowfin tuna) glazed and glistening in shoyu. These visions are appropriate to the poke served in Hawaiʻi today. However, I didn't grow up eating ʻahi poke at home. We had it from time to time, but in my house, our poke was gray. We ate humble enenue or sea chub, which is a reef fish, and we would use its light-gray flesh to make big batches of fresh poke on a regular basis. We also used white fish like papio (trevally) or uku (gray snapper). The point is, poke can be made with a wide variety of fish and seasoned in many ways. But shoyu poke is a staple in Hawaiʻi, and if you serve it on a bowl of hot white rice, you've got a poke bowl. Top it with some avocado or cucumber and sprinkle with sesame seeds, and now you're just getting fancy.

In a medium bowl, combine the shoyu, onion, sesame oil, sugar, ginger, chiles, and green onions, and stir to combine. Add the fish and stir gently to combine. Taste and adjust the seasoning. Transfer the poke to a medium serving bowl, then top with the avocado and cucumber, if using. Serve immediately, or cover and chill in the fridge for 1 hour to let the flavors mingle.

Do Ahead: *The poke can be made 1 day in advance of serving and stored, covered, in the fridge. Add the cucumber and avocado when ready to serve.*

Fish Alternatives

Aku (skipjack tuna)
Ono (wahoo)
Enenue (sea chub)

Island-Style Smoked Fish

Serves 6 to 8 as an appetizer

2 pounds boneless, skinless trevally fillet, or any medium to large fish

Smoked Fish Marinade

1 cup shoyu

¾ cup firmly packed light brown sugar

2 tablespoons toasted sesame oil

One 3-inch knob fresh ginger, peeled and finely minced

2 garlic cloves, smashed

2 fresh Hawaiian chiles or your hot chile of choice, minced

These candied little protein bars are another classic snack of Hawaiʻi. They are great to take on the go, to serve as pūpū, or to snack on with a cold beer. You can also mince them up and mix with mayo for a smoky fish spread. Smoking fish is a great way to preserve and extend the shelf life of any fish—a solid technique to use if you have an abundance of fish and not enough time to eat it all in its prime freshness. You don't need sashimi-grade fish to make this recipe as it lends itself to fish of all qualities. Tough fish, oily fish, fishy fish—by the time it's cut into strips, marinated overnight, and then kissed with smoke, it's a happy fish and a great snack.

Slice the fish fillets into roughly 4 by 1-inch-long strips.

To make the marinade: In a medium bowl, add the shoyu, brown sugar, sesame oil, ginger, garlic, and chiles. Stir to combine until the sugar dissolves.

Add the fish strips to the bowl, cover, and refrigerate for 8 hours or overnight.

When you are ready to cook, preheat your smoker to 165°F. Smoke for 3½ hours. The outside of the fish should be caramelized, but the inside should still be somewhat soft. Place the fish uncovered in the fridge to cool. Serve immediately or store, covered, in the fridge for up to 2 weeks.

Fish Alternatives

Marlin
ʻAhi
Snapper

Misoyaki Butterfish

Serves 4 to 6

2 pounds skin-on black cod fillets

1 cup packed light brown sugar

½ cup shoyu

¼ cup white miso paste

¼ cup rice vinegar

2 tablespoons freshly grated ginger

Butterfish is Hawai'i's loving nickname for black cod or sablefish. I'm not sure when black cod first made it to Hawai'i, but it's said that sugar plantation workers who migrated from Japan introduced this food to Hawai'i as well as the flavors of miso and shoyu. Misoyaki butterfish is a beloved delicacy still served at restaurants in Hawai'i today. It's sweet, fatty, and salty, and like the nickname suggests, when you take a bite, it melts like butter. Heads up—this recipe needs to marinate overnight but the flavor is well worth the wait.

With a sharp knife, cut the fish into roughly 2 by 4 by 1-inch pieces.

In a large mixing bowl, add the brown sugar, shoyu, miso, rice vinegar, and ginger, and stir until the sugar and the miso are thoroughly combined. Submerge the fish pieces in the marinade flesh-side down, cover, and refrigerate 8 hours or overnight.

Set the oven to broil on high heat. Line a baking sheet with parchment paper. Place the marinated fish pieces directly on the prepared baking sheet skin-side up. Cook until the skin is blistered and charred, about 6 minutes, then flip the fish and continue to cook for 4 minutes. Check the fish for doneness with a fork—the flesh should flake. If the fish isn't done, continue to broil for 1 more minute, then check it again. Remove the fish from the oven.

Serve immediately while warm, drizzling any of the sauce from the baking sheet over the fish. You can also serve it at room temperature, bento-style, in a lunchbox.

Country Stew

Serves 4 to 6

2 pounds beef chuck, or venison meat from the front quarter (such as shanks or chucks), cut into 2-inch cubes

Flaky sea salt and freshly ground black pepper

Olive oil for sautéing

1 yellow onion, chopped

4 ribs celery, chopped

4 carrots, scrubbed and chopped

3 garlic cloves, chopped

¼ cup tomato paste

3 tablespoons all-purpose flour

1 cup dry red wine

5 cups water

2 teaspoons Better Than Bouillon Roasted Chicken or Roasted Beef Base

3 dried bay leaves

3 cups 1-inch cubes peeled firm green ʻulu or Yukon Gold potatoes

1 tablespoon chopped fresh thyme

Note: *This recipe can be made up to 3 days in advance and reheated to serve.*

Hawaiʻi has a long-rooted history of cattle ranching with its own unique paniolo (Hawaiian cowboy) culture. And the American influence introduced the continental recipe of beef stew with carrots, celery, and potatoes, which has been loved and adored here ever since. It's a common meal served at dinner tables among local families or as a plate lunch option at restaurants. Common Hawaiʻi style garnishes for beef stew are a dollop of mayonnaise and a hit of chili pepper water. When I make this country-style stew, I usually replace the beef with stewing cuts of venison, and I love to sub out the potatoes for ʻulu (breadfruit). For me, it's about using what my environment provides—deer being an invasive species and ʻulu growing so abundantly that most people don't know what to do with their harvests. But whether it's beef or game, potatoes or ʻulu, a slow-cooked bowl of this paniolo classic is like a warm hug on a cold day.

Season the beef cubes with salt and pepper. In a large Dutch oven or a large, wide pot over medium-high heat, add enough olive oil to coat the bottom of the pot, and warm the oil. Working in batches, add the beef cubes to the pot in a single layer, making sure they are not overcrowded. Sear on each side until they turn golden brown, 5 to 7 minutes. Transfer to a plate and add more oil if necessary to sear the next batch.

Add all the beef back to the pot and stir in the onion. When the onion has softened, about 2 minutes, stir in the celery. After 2 minutes, add the carrots and the garlic. After 2 minutes, stir in the tomato paste until everything is well coated. Then add the flour, stir, and cook until the flour has browned, about 3 minutes. Stir in the wine, scraping any brown bits off the bottom of the pot. Add the water, bouillon base, and bay leaves. Bring to a boil and turn down the heat to low and simmer.

Cover and cook for 1½ hours, stirring occasionally to make sure nothing sticks to the bottom of the pot. Add more water to cover as needed. Add the ʻulu and the thyme and cook until the beef and ʻulu are fork-tender, another 20 minutes. Remove the bay leaves and serve immediately.

Eat the Invasives

Hawai'i is well known for its beauty and abundant biodiversity. So much so that I think people often don't realize that it is also dubbed the endangered and extinction capital of the world. The reason why Hawai'i has such a high rate of endangered species and extinction is because of habitat loss and invasive species. Many of the native species here are endemic to Hawai'i, meaning they can be found nowhere else in the world, so once they are gone, they are gone forever. Invasive species play a large role in decimating fragile native ecosystems. Now, not all introduced species become invasive—in fact, most remain quite harmless. But invasive species are nonnative species that cause immense harm to animal and plant life and alter an ecosystem by destroying its biodiversity—in short, not good.

But, as a chronic optimist, I always have to look on the bright side before truths like this get me too depressed. And one really bright side is that there are actually many invasive species we can eat! And so many of them are absolutely delicious. We have snapper (ta'ape and to'au) that our government brought in during the 1950s that have taken over the reefs and ocean floors, but they are a great food source. This could be a triple bottom-line win, giving us food security, boosting the local economy, and helping the native ecosystem—if more fishers targeted them.

Back in 2008, a group of my spearfishing friends on Maui started spearfishing tournaments on a grassroots level that targeted invasive fish only. It was an amazing movement to be a part of, and it set me on a new path of competing. It made me so proud that in 2023, when Hawai'i hosted the United States Spearfishing National Championships, it was announced that it would focus on invasive species only. I actually hadn't competed in a national championship for fifteen years, but my mentor Andy and I teamed up to celebrate this historic win.

The "Eat the Invasives" movement has moved well beyond fish. Local communities have taken this initiative into their own hands, and our hometown chefs have been the biggest warriors and heroes in supporting this change. I've attended everything from backyard gatherings to fancy-schmancy galas where communities and chefs harvest invasive plants and animals and plate them elegantly. And that's exactly why you see so many venison recipes throughout this book. Axis deer is one of the most prevalent invasive species on the islands of Maui, Lāna'i, and Moloka'i. Other invasive ungulates include sheep on the Big Island and goats and feral pigs on all the islands. Again, the positive side of this is that they are all absolutely delicious. And I think it's really important to still treat these animals as the gold they are when it comes to being top-notch quality food. My friend Ku'uipo, a taro farmer and educator with the biggest heart in the world, likes to remind young students that it's not the fault of the plants or animals that they ended up here. It's usually a result of human action. So, rather than call them "invasive," she calls them "displaced." And I'll never forget the witty eight-year-old Aki, who responded to Ku'uipo with such enthusiasm: "If they're displaced, I can place them! In my belly!" I couldn't agree more.

Chef Hui
Paepae o He‘eia
He‘eia Fishpond, He‘eia, O‘ahu

Meat Jun

(Battered Pan-Fried Venison)

Serves 4 to 6

1 pound venison meat from the hindquarter (such as rump roast or sirloin) or beef sirloin chuck roast, sliced very thinly against the grain

2 teaspoons baking soda

½ cup shoyu

¼ cup white vinegar

¼ cup granulated sugar

1 tablespoon toasted sesame oil

2 garlic cloves, chopped

1 cup all-purpose flour

4 eggs, beaten

Avocado oil for frying

Meat Jun Sauce

½ cup shoyu

¼ cup plus 1 tablespoon white vinegar

1 tablespoon toasted sesame oil

1 tablespoon granulated sugar

1 teaspoon Crunchy Garlic Chili Oil (page 191, optional)

1 garlic clove, chopped

Coarsely ground black pepper

Meat jun is a menu item at every Korean restaurant in Hawaiʻi. Therefore, I always assumed it was Korean. Turns out it's not actually from Korea—instead, it's a Korean-Hawaiʻi fusion food that was created here in the islands. It's made with thinly sliced meat coated in flour and then dipped in egg before being pan-fried. The result is a soft, spongy coating rather than a super crispy one. That spongy outside is made for being completely submerged in a tangy vinegar-shoyu sauce that absorbs it perfectly.

Lay the venison slices flat on a cutting board and sprinkle the baking soda over both sides of the slices. Then place them in a bowl and massage to distribute the baking soda. Cover the bowl with a towel or plate and let it sit for 25 to 30 minutes in the fridge. (The use of baking soda is a "velveting" technique to tenderize the meat.) Rinse the venison slices under cold running water and reserve.

In a medium bowl, combine the shoyu, vinegar, sugar, sesame oil, and garlic.

Add the venison and mix well to coat all the pieces (don't miss any folds or crevices!). Cover and marinate in the fridge for 1 hour.

Place a wire rack over a baking pan and set near the stove. Place the flour and eggs into separate shallow dishes. In a large skillet over medium-high heat, warm ¼ inch of avocado oil until hot. Working in batches, shake the marinade off a slice of venison and dredge it in the flour, then in the beaten egg. Gently add the coated meat to the skillet, cook until golden brown, about 3 minutes, then flip and repeat on the other side. Transfer the meat to the prepared wire rack to cool. Repeat with the rest of the meat.

To make the sauce: In a small bowl, mix the shoyu, vinegar, sesame oil, sugar, garlic chili oil (if using), garlic, and several grindings of pepper. Stir until the sugar dissolves.

Cut the meat pieces horizontally into 1-inch strips and serve with the sauce.

The humble fish that raised me.

Popcorn-Style Fried Octopus

Serves 10 as an appetizer

2 pounds octopus, innards removed, previously frozen for at least 4 days, and defrosted

2 tablespoons coarse sea salt

Neutral oil for frying

2 cups all-purpose flour

½ cup granulated garlic

Flaky sea salt

Fried heʻe (octopus)—the popcorn of the sea—is insanely addicting. I fell in love with fried heʻe the first time I met it on the pūpū buffet line at a casual outdoor wedding and have loved it at every party where I've encountered it since then. It's a special treat when someone brings fried heʻe to a gathering, and it always goes fast. Many people pressure-cook or parboil their octopus first to tenderize it, then cut it up and bread it for a quick fry. But my favorite fried heʻe recipe comes from a rugged and wise fisherman named Uncle Billy, and there was no parcooking involved. He taught me that you must take the time to freeze your octopus for at least a few days, and you must take the time to thoroughly massage it once it has defrosted. You also want to cut your octopus into small bite-size pieces. It will still be a slightly chewier version than the parboiled style, but it's a nice chew and the octopus flavor is more concentrated and simply out of this world. Uncle Billy also taught me to add granulated garlic to my flour. It adds the perfect punch to the crunch.

Put the defrosted octopus in a large mixing bowl and sprinkle with the coarse salt. Use your hands to vigorously squeeze, push, and press the entire octopus for 7 minutes—think of it as a deep tissue massage. At the thicker parts of the legs and head, apply pressure as you squeeze. Thoroughly rinse the octopus in cold running water. It will foam somewhat; keep rinsing until all the suds are gone and the water runs clear.

Place the cleaned octopus on a cutting board. Remove some of the excess moisture by wiping it with a paper towel (it's okay if it's a little wet). Cut the head off above the eyes (where the head narrows), then cut below the eyes about 1½ inches down from the first cut. Discard the section with the eyes, but keep the rest.

To remove the beak, make an incision from where the two legs meet toward the center of the octopus until you reach a hard black piece (the beak). Remove it and discard. Use the knife to separate the eight legs. Cut each leg by starting at the thickest part and slice into ¼-inch pieces. As the leg gets skinnier, make your slices a little wider to make them roughly even in size. Toward the skinniest part of the leg, cut the slices almost 1 inch in length. For the head, slice it open and spread it out so it's one flat piece, then cut into ¼-inch strips.

In a large skillet over medium-high heat, warm 1 inch of oil.

continued

Stuffed Uhu

continued

incisions and cavity. Flip the fish and repeat on the other side, starting with the remaining sauce, then the remaining toppings. Stuff in any vegetables or sausage that fell out underneath the fish or mound them on top. (This takes the word *stuffed* to a whole other level—you want a heaping avalanche of fillings.) Top with the other ti leaf, then another 24 inches of foil, shiny-side up. Fold and crimp the edges of both pieces of foil together, rolling them in toward the fish until all four sides are completely sealed and tight to the fish.

If you're cooking in an oven, place the foil-wrapped fish on a baking sheet, then place in the oven. If you're cooking over a grill, place the foil-wrapped fish directly on the grate.

Cook for 30 minutes, then check the fish for doneness. If you can poke a wooden chopstick or knife through the thickest part, making sure the thickest part can lift off the bone, it's ready. If not, seal the foil back up and put the fish back in the oven or on the grill for 5 minutes at a time until it's ready. Serve immediately.

Grandma's ʻŌpelu

(Dried Baitfish)

Serves 4 to 6

6 ʻōpelu (mackerel scad), about 4 ounces each, scaled and gutted

Flaky sea salt

Chili Pepper Water (page 34) for serving

Poi (page 177) for serving

My sister Christy reviewed a draft of this book, and immediately exclaimed, "What about Grandma's dried pulehu ʻōpelu?!" I had forgotten how much she loved eating salty little baitfish as a kid and how she would sit with my grandma by a small fire, picking the charred fish to the bone. I explained to my sister that most people don't eat baitfish or have an old-school fish-drying box, but soon after I happened to catch a handful of ʻōpelu. I butterflied and dried my catch and drove to Christy's home in Waiʻanae. She made a fire and we grilled these little fish and dipped them in chili pepper water. The smell of smoke in the air took us to a nostalgic place of appreciation as we savored every salty bite. This day together made me understand that this recipe deserves to live on.

Two days before you plan to serve it, start preparing the fish for drying. To butterfly the fish, place an ʻōpelu on a cutting board horizontally with the belly side facing you. Starting from the gut cavity, use a sharp knife to cut horizontally to the tail as if you were filleting the fish (see page 245), cutting through the spine but leaving the back ridge intact. Make similar fillet-style cuts in the opposite direction, from the gut cavity to the mouth, until the entire fish can be split open, connected only by the back ridge. Repeat with the remaining fish.

With the skin-side up, lay the open fish on the cutting board. Make 3 to 4 diagonal incisions 1 inch apart, then repeat in the opposite direction to score the skin. Repeat with the remaining fish. Season both sides of the fish with salt.

If you're using a drying box in dry, sunny, warm weather: Place the fish skin-side down on the rack of the drying box, making sure to leave space in between so that the fish are not touching one another. Close the drying box and leave it out in the sun and wind all day. Remove the fish from the drying box at the end of the day, store in a paper bag in the fridge overnight, and then repeat the drying process the next day, skin-side up. The fish are ready when both sides have a shiny, leathery appearance. Store the dried fish in a paper bag in the fridge until ready to grill.

If you're using a food dehydrator: Preheat the dehydrator to 130° to 150°F. Place the fish on the rack and dehydrate for 6 to 8 hours. Remove the fish.

To grill the fish: Preheat a grill to high heat (400°F). Place the dried fish on the grill and cook until they develop a nice char, roughly 3 minutes, then flip and repeat on the other side. Serve with chili pepper water and poi.

Fish Alternatives

Akule (bigeye scad)
Sardines
Mackerel

Family-Style Laulau

Serves 4

½-pound skin-on black cod (defrosted if previously frozen)

Coarse sea salt

½-pound boneless venison meat from the front shoulder or shank or boneless pork butt, cut into 2-inch chunks

8 ti leaves (optional)

20 medium lūʻau (taro leaves) or 12 large collard leaves (about 1 pound), stems removed and reserved

½ pound kalo (taro root) or ½ pound sweet potato, peeled and cubed into 8 pieces

Laulau means "bundle," and these delicious bundles of meat, fish, and greens are a true backbone of Hawaiʻi's cuisine. Laulau is traditionally cooked in an imu (an underground oven) and is usually made in mass quantities. Digging and preparing an imu is a lot of work and cooking food in it is an all-day or overnight process—so if you're going to go through the effort to make laulau this way, it makes sense to make a lot. It's usually a community event; people stand in factory assembly-style lines, with someone stacking leaves, someone adding meat, someone adding fish, someone wrapping. The final result is usually served at big parties or lūʻau or even sold at kids' school or sporting fundraisers. Laulau is delicious, fatty, salty fish and meat surrounded by smoky leafy greens, served with poi and chili pepper water; there's nothing else like it. This recipe is for small-batch laulau at home. I use an electric pressure cooker instead of an imu, which makes it so easy and saves a lot of cooking time. I usually use venison instead of beef since that's what I have on hand, but laulau can also be made using pork or chicken.

The day before you plan to serve, start preparing the fish. In a medium bowl, sprinkle 1 tablespoon of salt over the fish. Cover and let sit in the fridge overnight.

The next day, remove the fish from the bowl, rinse under cold running water, and cut into four pieces.

Generously season the meat with salt.

To assemble the laulau: Set up a workstation at a counter or table. If you're using ti leaves, it's best to remove their stiff central ribs (see photo in the top left corner on page 158). (If you don't have ti leaves, you can use aluminum foil instead.) Flip the leaves over so they are rib-side up. One third from the tip of the leaf, hold your knife at a slight angle toward the base of the leaf and make a shallow incision in the rib, making sure to not cut all the way through the leaf. Position the leaf so the incision is at the edge of a counter or table, bend the leaf at the incision, then slide the top of the leaf away from you while pressing against the table to make the hard part of the rib peel off. Repeat with the remaining ti leaves.

Fish Alternatives

Lingcod
Enenue (sea chub)
Salmon

continued

Family-Style Laulau

continued

Cut the lūʻau stems into 1-inch pieces, then divide into four piles.

Stack five lūʻau leaves. Place two pieces of kalo, one-quarter of the meat, one piece of fish, and one pile of lūʻau stems in the center of the lūʻau leaves. Fold the bottom of the lūʻau leaves over the filling, then fold the sides in, then tightly roll the laulau to the top. Pin the open part down by turning it over.

If you are using ti leaves, take two ti leaves and arrange them in an X shape, overlapping each other. Place the laulau in the center. Fold all the ends of the ti leaves up around the laulau. Using the two stem pieces, wrap them around the neck of the leaves just over the laulau, and tie in a knot to enclose.

If you're using aluminum foil, cut a piece 16 to 18 inches long. Place the laulau in the center of the foil and fold the foil over it to encase it.

In the pot of an electric pressure cooker with a rack inserted, add 2 cups of water and the laulau. Lock the lid into place and cook on high pressure for 2 hours. Manually release the pressure. Once the steam has released, remove the laulau. Unwrap the laulau, discarding the ti leaf or foil, and serve immediately.

Oxtail Lūʻau Stew

Serves 4 to 6

Olive oil for sautéing

2 pounds beef oxtail or pork shoulder, cut into 2-inch pieces

Flaky sea salt and freshly ground black pepper

1 yellow onion, chopped

2 garlic cloves, chopped

One 3-inch knob fresh ginger, peeled and minced

5 cups chicken broth

1½ pounds lūʻau (taro) leaves or Swiss chard, stems removed and roughly chopped

Cooked white rice or Poi (page 177) for serving

Chili Pepper Water (page 34) for serving

Lūʻau stew is like the liquid stovetop version of a laulau (see page 156)—a classic Hawaiian dish—a bundle of meat and salted fish wrapped in lūʻau (taro) leaves and steamed. It's basically a bowl of warm green comfort. Unlike squid lūʻau, which has a strong, sweet coconut-milk presence, my meat lūʻau is savory and brothy. Many different meats can be used to make lūʻau stew. I usually use the front shoulder or tougher cuts of venison with sinew, which, as they cook down, become tender and emulate fat. But one day I found a package of beef oxtails in my freezer and used that instead. Winnah!

In a large pot over medium-high heat, add enough olive oil to coat the bottom of the pot, and warm the oil. Season the oxtail pieces with salt and pepper. Working in batches, place them in a single layer in the pot so they aren't touching. Cook, letting the pieces brown on each side before flipping them to cook the other side, about 5 minutes total. Add the onion to the pan, stir, and cook for 2 minutes. Add the garlic and ginger, stir, and cook for another 2 minutes. Add the chicken broth and lūʻau leaves, cover, and bring to a boil. Then turn down the heat to medium-low and let simmer, covered, for 2 hours. Check the stew occasionally and give it a little stir to make sure the leaves are submerged and nothing is sticking to the bottom of the pot.

After 2 hours, use wooden chopsticks or a fork to start pulling the meat away from the bones. (I usually serve it with the bones but you can remove them if you want.) Taste and season with salt and pepper. Cook for an additional 30 minutes covered. Serve immediately over rice or with poi and chili pepper water.

5

Buddy

Cooking for My Son

Since I was a young girl, I knew I wanted to be a mom one day. In my twenties, I didn't feel ready because I didn't have a real career or financial stability. In my thirties, I met Justin right when my career in diving started to take off, which consisted of adventure after adventure so becoming a mom was put on hold further. When we finally decided we were ready to make a family and spend more time at home, I was thirty-nine, and things happened almost instantly as we were blessed with a little boy who we named Buddy.

As I write this book, Buddy is five years old. He questions authority, loves repeating any bad words he hears, and has more sass than I know what to do with. He loves to paint and create art. He loves fishing and, fortunately for me, he has always been a good eater.

Now don't get me wrong, there are plenty of times when Buddy isn't feeling like eating. Or when he's just in a mood and decides he's going to snub my food for no apparent reason. But the main thing that gets him curious about trying food is experiencing the magic of where it comes from and being a part of the process of cooking it.

Cooking with a young child is like trying to run with a parachute on. It's gonna slow you down. It is neither efficient nor peaceful. I'm constantly watching what his little hands are touching, how big of a mess he is making, and how close he is to hurting himself. It's a lot to manage while trying to get a meal made. But it's absolutely worth it. I've had to scoop out the handful of salt Buddy threw into my batter when I asked for a pinch. I've had to use extreme patience when he wrecked my neatly arranged mise en place because he was playing drums on the ingredients with the wooden spoons. And he's definitely learned the consequence of hot pans when helping me at the stovetop. As I write this, I feel the stress creeping in on me, but I also remember him eating his own homemade pasta noodles or slurping down menpachi miso soup with an extra sense of appreciation for the work he put into it. And if there's any skill I can give him, knowing how to cook will make him a capable human in life.

I'm proud that he has an understanding of where his meals come from. I love that when he eats meat, he truly understands that he is eating an animal from nature. I love that when I go diving, he will put in orders for his favorite dinners the same way I did with my dad. And thanks to Justin's gardening, he has the same appreciation for the plants that feed us.

Since having Buddy, I find myself putting more time into cooking food with local whole ingredients. Having someone to cook for, although at times a chore, also feels like an opportunity for me to practice my passion and express my love. These recipes have been some of Buddy's favorite meals in his early years of life so far, and we've prepared many of them together.

YETI

Fried Fish

Serves 4

8 to 10 small whole fish, such as āholehole, menpachi, manini, or kole (see Note)
Hawaiian sea salt or flaky sea salt
Freshly ground black pepper
Neutral oil for frying
Chili Pepper Water for serving (page 34)

Note: *Each fish should be no bigger than 1 pound. If you have larger fish, cut them into pieces that are less than 1 pound.*

Some of my first memories are of eating small fried fish with my family, humble but delicious fish that don't get much bigger than the length of a shaka (five to six inches). Āholehole, menpachi, manini, and kole, all speared by my dad, were cleaned whole in our backyard in Maui, never filleted. We would eat these fried fish whole, dipped into chili pepper water—a spicy vinegar sauce. As kids, it was fun to eat the crispy fins and entire tail like a potato chip. Grandma always encouraged us to eat the eyeballs and would say eating them makes us "akamai" or smart. These are the fish that I consider to be the root of my upbringing.

These are the same fish that awoke something in me and brought me back to diving as an adult. The ones they don't serve at restaurants that reminded me of the values I was taught as a kid. And today, fried fish is one of Buddy's favorite meals.

Every time I go diving, he puts in his orders for menpachi and other small fish that can be fried whole. He catches his own lunch for preschool with a little bamboo pole off the jetty of the harbor—usually little toʻau, invasive snappers in Hawaiʻi—that he brings to school the next day with stories for his teachers. He likes to nibble on the tail and fins just as I did. And like my grandma, he chews on the eyeballs. Simple fried fish is still a favorite meal for my family and me. And if by the end of this whole book, you simply walk away knowing how to scale, gut, score, season, and fry a fish whole to feed yourselves or serve to someone you care about, well, that's a legacy of love worth giving.

Scale and gut the fish (see page 244). Rinse the fish and pat them dry with paper towels or a cloth (you want the fish to be dry so that the oil doesn't splatter during frying). With a sharp knife, cut 3 deep diagonal slits on both sides of the fish 1 inch apart. The slits should be deep enough to expose the flesh but not down to the bone. Make a couple slits going the other direction diagonally on each side as well. Generously season the fish with salt and pepper, then set them aside while you prepare the cooking oil.

continued

Fish Alternatives

Crappie
Scup
Rockfish

Fried Fish

continued

Place a wire rack over a baking pan and set near the stove. Pour ¼-inch of oil into a large skillet (cast iron is ideal) over medium-high heat. Make sure you are in a well-ventilated area and turn on your stove's exhaust fan—it can get smoky. The oil is ready for frying when you dip a fish tail in and the oil sizzles, about 3 minutes. Carefully place the entire fish in the oil and cook until the skin turns crispy and golden, 3 to 4 minutes, depending on the thickness of the fish. Using cooking chopsticks or tongs, flip and cook until the edges of the knife cuts turn golden brown, 2 to 3 minutes.

Using tongs, transfer the fish to the prepared wire racks to cool. (If you are using tongs, I suggest keeping them angled slightly downward, as hot oil can funnel down the inside channels of the tool and dangerously onto one's hands!) Serve immediately with chili pepper water for dipping. When the fish are cool enough, eating with your hands is encouraged.

Buddy's Fried Rice

Serves 4 to 6

Olive oil for sautéing

1½ cups chopped Portuguese sausage or any protein of your choice, such as leftover cooked fish or meat, bacon, smoked fish, or smoked meat

½ cup chopped yellow onion

1 carrot, scrubbed and finely chopped

½ cup chopped greens, such as Swiss chard or bok choy (optional)

10 green beans, chopped (optional)

4 button mushrooms, coarsely chopped (optional)

3 garlic cloves, minced

3 tablespoons toasted sesame oil

4 cups cooked rice, plus more as needed, preferably at least 1 day old

Flaky sea salt and freshly ground black pepper

3 tablespoons shoyu, plus more for serving

1 tablespoon oyster sauce

Juice of ½ lime

2 eggs

½ cup roughly chopped fresh cilantro

1 bunch green onions, white and green parts, chopped

Chili Pepper Water (page 34) for serving

I make fried rice often for Buddy. He loves it, and it's a great way to clean out the fridge. It almost feels wrong to write a recipe because I rarely make it the same. That's because the entire essence of fried rice is using what I have on hand. For protein, I might have summer sausage, chorizo, a leftover roast, fish, or smoked meat. Then I dig through the veggie drawer and include anything from asparagus to bok choy. And depending how much I have of each ingredient, the ratios change often. Sometimes I add eggs; other days I don't. Sometimes I finish with fresh lime juice; other days I use oyster sauce. My main rule of thumb is to use rice that is at least a day old so it doesn't get mushy when you stir it; start with your protein, onions, and any other hard vegetables; and make sure to salt it well whether you use salt, shoyu, or fish sauce. And throw in green onions and black pepper. Below is a recipe from the day we decided to write down what I do using what I had available, but remember: Anything goes. Meat is meat, sauce is sauce, veg is veg.

In a large skillet over medium-high heat, add enough olive oil to coat the bottom of the skillet, and warm the oil. Add the sausage, yellow onion, and carrots and stir. Once the onion begins to soften, about 2 minutes, add the greens (if using), green beans (if using), mushrooms (if using), and garlic. Continue to cook, stirring occasionally. After all the veggies become soft, about 3 minutes, add the sesame oil and continue to stir. After another 3 minutes, add 1 tablespoon of olive oil and then the rice. The rice will clump up when you first put it in the pan and form clusters, but keep stirring to break those up. When the rice starts crackling on the bottom of the skillet, add more oil if needed and scrape up the rice with a wooden spoon. Season with salt and a hefty amount of pepper, and cook for an additional 4 minutes. Turn down the heat to low, add the shoyu, oyster sauce, and lime juice, and stir with a wooden spoon, scraping the bottom of the skillet. Taste and adjust the seasoning.

Make a well in the middle of the pan by pushing the rice mixture to the sides. Pour a little olive oil into the well. Crack the eggs into the well. Pan-scramble the eggs with a spatula or fork and let the egg cook. When the egg is cooked but still runny, 3 to 4 minutes, fold it into the rice mixture along with the cilantro and green onions. Serve immediately or at room temperature, with shoyu and chili pepper water on the side to drizzle.

23

Poi

Makes 4 cups

1 pound kalo (taro root), peeled and chopped into 1-inch cubes

3½ cups water, plus more for thinning

I always imagined Buddy's first solid food would be poi. It's a common first food for babies in Hawai'i and an absolute foundation of Hawaiian cuisine. I couldn't wait until Buddy was six months old so I could finally feed it to him. Poi is cooked kalo (taro root) traditionally pounded with water until it's gooey. For people who didn't grow up on poi, it can be a hard sell. Some call it bland or say it tastes like glue. But to me, poi tastes like the subtly sweet flavors of the earth itself.

One day when Buddy was four months old, Justin and I were out diving with our friends Kapua Kawelo and Joby Rohrer. It was really hard as a mom with a newborn baby to go diving since I needed to breastfeed every couple of hours. I couldn't just strap him to me and bring him along on a swim, or leave him on a boat all day while I was underwater. Joby and Kapua made diving possible for Justin and me during those times as brand-new parents, and for that, I will always be grateful.

With Buddy strapped to her, Kapua would captain the boat. When Buddy got hungry, Kapua would zoom in like a pro to scoop me out of the ocean to breastfeed. With boobs relieved and Buddy content, she'd plop me back in the water to catch up with the guys. We always joked that I needed a more nursing-friendly wetsuit.

But on this day, I realized my underwater session was lasting longer than usual. I was grateful. But eventually those intrusive mom voices of concern started quacking at me. I poked my head out of the water and called the boat over. Kapua, with Buddy strapped to her, leaned over the rail and peeked back at me. Buddy had the biggest smile with muted purple paste all over his face. "Holy cow! He loves poi!" Kapua exclaimed. I chuckled and I put my head back in the water, as I do not question Kapua's ability in caring for babies. Later, Kapua proudly raved about what a great eater Buddy was. She snickered at how weird people have gotten with "the silly idea" that babies have to be six months old before being eating real food. Justin and I both nodded our heads—"so weird." And just like that poi became—and still is—one of Buddy's favorite meals!

Add the kalo and 2 cups of the water to the pot of an electric pressure cooker. Lock the lid into place and cook on high pressure for 1 hour. Manually release the pressure. When the steam has released from the pressure cooker, remove the lid and, using a long spoon, scoop the kalo into a blender. Add the remaining 1½ cups of water to the blender, cover, and blend on high speed until smooth, adding more water if the poi begins to stick to the sides of the blender. I like my poi to be one stage thicker than coating the back of a spoon. Serve immediately with foods that have punchy, salty flavors, like fried fish or cured and smoked meat (page 97).

Note: *You can freeze prepared poi, then heat it gently over medium-low heat on the stove with ½ cup of water for each cup of poi to reconstitute.*

Menpachi Miso Soup

Serves 4 to 6

1½ pounds whole menpachi (3 medium or 2 large fish), scaled, gilled, and gutted (see page 244)

One 2-inch knob fresh ginger, peeled and thinly sliced

Fine sea salt

2 tablespoons salted butter

⅛ medium yellow onion, sliced thinly, then cut into 2-inch pieces

1 cup sliced fresh shiitake, oyster, or button mushrooms

3 garlic cloves, minced

½ cup white miso, plus more as needed

¼ cup mirin

6 green onions, white and green parts, chopped

2 tablespoons dried cut wakame

2 to 3 cups cooked white rice (optional)

7 ounces medium-firm tofu, cut into ½-inch cubes (optional)

Menpachi is Buddy's favorite fish. The only way I've ever known to eat it is fried whole. But I've heard stories from different dive partners over the years about their grandmas making menpachi miso soup. Buddy's love for this fish led me to wanting more ways to prepare these sweet little delicacies, so I finally gave it a try and absolutely loved it. This soup is so quick and easy, and it's fun to let Buddy help me make it. Rockfish would be a great substitute! I suggest getting the broth started and then mincing the veggies to save time.

With a sharp knife, carve the fish fillets from the body of the fish (see page 245), reserving the bones and head. Menpachi has an extra row of bones in the top quarter of its fillet, so you will need to find these bones and trim them out as well. Cut the boneless fillets into bite-size pieces (1½ to 2 inches, as the fish will shrink when cooked) and reserve.

In a medium pot, combine the fish head and bones and the ginger. Add enough water to cover. Put a lid on the pot, bring to a boil over medium-high heat, then turn down the heat to medium-low and simmer for 15 to 20 minutes. Strain the liquid through a spider or a colander into a glass or stainless-steel bowl, reserving the fish broth. Discard the fish head, bones, and ginger.

Lightly season the fish pieces with salt. I like to check the pieces again here for any small bones I might have missed and remove them with a sharp knife if necessary. Place the fish pieces on a plate or a cutting board and reserve.

In a medium pot over medium heat, melt the butter. Add the onion and cook, stirring occasionally, until the onion begins to soften, about 2 minutes. Add the mushrooms and continue to cook, stirring occasionally, 2 to 3 minutes. Then add the garlic and cook for 1 additional minute. Season with a pinch of salt. Add the miso and 1 cup of the fish broth, and stir to incorporate the miso. Add the rest of the fish broth and the mirin. Taste and add more miso if necessary. (I look for a balance of miso flavor without the broth getting too salty.) Cook for an additional 3 minutes to let the flavors mingle; then add the green onions (but reserve 1 tablespoon for garnish) and wakame. Bring the soup to a simmer, then remove from the heat.

Set out serving bowls. Add ½ cup of warm rice to each bowl, if using. Divide the raw fish and tofu (if using) among the bowls. Ladle the piping-hot soup over the fish, making sure to scoop up some of the veggies and wakame for each bowl. (Because the soup is blazing hot, by the time it's cool enough to eat, it will have perfectly cooked the fish.) Garnish with the remaining 1 tablespoon of green onions and serve immediately.

Smoked 'Ahi Bacon Pasta

Serves 4 to 6

1 recipe Handmade Pasta (recipe follows), or 1 pound dried spaghetti or linguine

Olive oil for sautéing

1 cup diced Cured and Smoked Fish, preferably 'ahi (see page 97) or cooked diced bacon

¼ cup salted butter

8 ounces king oyster, button, or cremini mushrooms, thinly sliced

Flaky sea salt

3 garlic cloves, finely minced or microplaned

Zest and juice from 1 lemon, plus more for garnishing

Freshly ground black pepper

1 cup heavy cream

1 cup grated Parmigiano-Reggiano cheese, plus more for garnishing

Minced fresh flat-leaf parsley for garnishing (optional)

Red pepper flakes (optional)

I love having cured, smoked fish on hand. I've found that when I crisp it up in a pan, it becomes a super delicious fish bacon. And that bacon, combined with garlic, lemon zest, and cream achieves next-level, decadent pasta sauce. The key to perfection is to taste as you season, making sure that every bite will be hit with love from salt and pepper. This dish tastes simple but sophisticated, and it is one that kids love just as much as the adults do. When I am feeling brave, Buddy and I will make handmade pasta, but if I am short on time, dried spaghetti or linguine will work, and the whole dish can be made in minutes!

In a large pot, cook the pasta to recipe or package directions. Strain into a colander, reserving ¾ cup pasta water. Drizzle the cooked pasta with olive oil, toss lightly to evenly coat, and reserve.

Meanwhile, in a medium skillet over medium-high heat, add enough olive oil to coat the bottom of the skillet, and warm the oil. Add the cured 'ahi and cook, stirring occasionally so that it doesn't stick to the skillet and burn. When the edges are browned and crispy, about 5 minutes, remove the skillet from the heat and reserve.

Return the pasta pot to the stove and, over medium-high heat, melt the butter. Add the mushrooms, season with salt, and stir. When the mushrooms are soft, about 3 minutes, lower the heat to medium-low. Add the garlic and the lemon zest, and stir. Cook for 1 minute, then stir in the lemon juice. Add the pasta to the pot and give it a stir to coat all the pasta with the lemon-garlic mixture. I like to season it with salt and pepper at this point and then adjust the seasoning again at the end. Raise the heat to medium and stir in the reserved pasta water and the cream. Bring to a simmer and cook, letting the liquid reduce until it thickens slightly, about 2 minutes. Stir in the cheese and turn off the heat.

To serve, pile a portion of pasta on a plate, season again with salt and pepper, and garnish with more cheese, parsley (if using), red pepper flakes (if using), and a squeeze of lemon juice. Top with the cooked 'ahi, and serve immediately.

Handmade Pasta

Makes 1 pound

2 cups all-purpose flour, plus more for dusting

3 eggs

Fine sea salt

1 teaspoon olive oil

In a large bowl, add the flour and push it into a large mound. Then make a large well in the center of the mound, pushing the flour toward the sides. Crack the eggs into the well and add 1 teaspoon salt and the olive oil. Using a fork, whisk the eggs together in the well to combine the salt and oil. Swap the fork for a wooden spoon and gently incorporate the surrounding flour into the egg mixture until it's all thoroughly combined into a rough ball.

Lightly dust your work surface with flour. Knead the dough for 4 to 5 minutes. When you poke the dough, it should spring back. Cover it and let it rest for 30 minutes.

Cut the dough into four pieces. Working in batches on the floured surface, knead the small balls four times to wake them up. Using a rolling pin, roll each ball as thinly as you possibly can; try for less than ⅛ of an inch. Dust the rolled pasta with flour, then loosely roll or fold the dough and cut it crosswise into ¼-inch slices. Unravel the strands and put them in a pile.

Bring a large pot of salted water to a boil over medium-high heat. Add the pasta and cook for 4 minutes. Drain the pasta in a colander. (If you're making this for Smoked 'Ahi Bacon Pasta (see previous page), reserve ¾ cup pasta water.)

Turmeric Ginger Bone Broth

Serves 4

4 cups Bone Broth (recipe follows)

One 4-inch knob fresh ginger, chopped or grated

One 4-inch piece fresh turmeric, chopped or grated

2 garlic cloves, chopped

Fine sea salt and freshly ground black pepper

Lime or lemon wedges for squeezing

My favorite way to start the morning is with a mug of hot bone broth, with all the flavors and medicinal benefits of garlic, turmeric, and ginger infused into it and finished with a generous squeeze of fresh citrus. I drink this before my cup of coffee and let it coat my stomach and supercharge my day. When Buddy was just two years old, I offered him a little mug of it one morning and he loved it. I remember watching him slowly wake up as he sipped the broth, saying "ahhhh" after every sip. He looked so much like a little old man drinking coffee and taking in the morning. He still won't pass up a mug of broth and neither will I.

Add the bone broth, ginger, turmeric, and garlic to a small pot, and bring to a boil over medium-high heat. Turn down the heat to medium-low and simmer for 5 minutes. Strain the liquid through a fine-mesh strainer into mugs. Season with salt, pepper, and a squeeze of lime, and serve.

Bone Broth

Makes 10 to 12 cups

5 pounds beef bones or venison or sheep bones, cut into 4-inch pieces (use a reciprocal saw or ask your butcher to cut them for you)

Olive oil for coating

Coarse sea salt and freshly ground black pepper

I make bone broth anytime I have bones on hand. I use it as a drinkable broth and as a stock for cooking. It keeps in the fridge for up to 1 week or in the freezer for 6 months. Heads up, the total prep time is 8 to 12 hours, so plan accordingly.

Preheat the oven to 450°F. Place the bones on a sheet tray or a roasting pan and lightly coat with olive oil. Season with salt and pepper. Place the tray in the oven and roast until the bones are crackling and spitting, and the meat is a rich brown, 30 minutes.

Add the roasted bones to a large pot and add enough water to cover them by 1 inch. Cover the pot with a lid and cook over medium-high heat. When it comes to a boil, turn down the heat to low and simmer for 8 to 10 hours. Check on the broth occasionally, adding more water if the level gets too low. Turn off the heat.

When the broth is cool, skim the solidified fat from the surface. Remove the bones and ladle the broth into a jar or container to store.

6

Rolling Solo

Simple Recipes for One (or More)

GEAR
SUPPLY

Justin has taken Buddy to visit family back in Minnesota a handful of times while I've stayed home in Hawai'i to work or just take a break from the daily duties of being a mom. It is absolutely mind-blowing how much my cooking changes the second my guys are out the door. I spend so much time thinking about what I can feed them for breakfast, lunch, and dinner and how to keep the household food inventory in a well-functioning flow. That all shuts down as soon as I drop them off at the airport.

I basically become the most low-maintenance bachelor you can imagine. Sometimes I'll go to a local pub solo and thoroughly enjoy a basket of mediocre buffalo wings and a cold, crisp IPA for dinner, just to flex how little of a fuss I'm going to put into making a meal. But for the most part, I still want to take good care of myself and eat fresh, wholesome food. I just don't want to overthink it, spend too much time on it, or go to the store. So, these recipes are made from the fresh staples I almost always have on hand or ingredients that are usually in my freezer or pantry, ready and begging to be whipped up into a quick and easy meal. These dishes are simple and delicious and make me feel like the queen of my own alone-time universe.

These recipes aren't exclusively for a party of one, though. They are nonfussy, quick, easy meals that can be shared and scaled up for more.

Queen of my alone-time universe.

Fancy Sardines and Crunchy Garlic Chili Oil

Serves 2 (or more)

Two 3.5-ounce tins preserved sardines, smoked oysters, or anchovies in olive oil

Fancy crackers

Handful of salad greens

Flaky sea salt and freshly ground black pepper

Parmigiano-Reggiano cheese for grating

Olive oil for drizzling

Lemon wedge for squeezing

Something pickled or preserved, such as pickled onion, pickled veggies or peppers, olives, and capers

½ cup sour cream

Crunchy Garlic Chili Oil (recipe follows)

Homemade chili oil is a great way to elevate any meal—even the most simple no-cook pantry meal I make when I'm on my own: fancy sardines on crackers. I always keep a stash of tinned fish on hand—sardines in tomatoes, smoked oysters, anchovies in olive oil—along with everything else on this list, but think of the ingredients listed here as loose suggestions. If you don't have one, don't go out and buy it—I wouldn't—just sub in something else.

Open the tins of preserved fish and place them on a large serving board alongside the crackers. On another side of the serving board, place the salad greens and sprinkle with salt, pepper, and grated Parmigiano-Reggiano cheese. Then drizzle the greens with some olive oil and a squeeze of lemon. Add the pickled or preserved items to the board. In a small bowl add a couple of big dollops of sour cream and top with a spoonful or two of the garlic chili oil. Place the bowl on the serving board. To eat, I'll put a nice scoop of sour cream with chili oil on a cracker (and admire how beautiful that is), and take turns with the toppings.

Crunchy Garlic Chili Oil

Makes 1½ cups

1 cup avocado oil

Cloves from 1 head of garlic, finely chopped

¼ cup crushed red pepper flakes

2 tablespoons granulated sugar

1 tablespoon paprika

2 teaspoons cayenne pepper

2 teaspoons fine sea salt

¼ cup toasted sesame oil

Aside from a charcuterie board, I love garlic chili oil on dumplings, ramen, and even sashimi.

In a medium skillet over medium-low heat, warm the avocado oil. Add the garlic and cook, stirring occasionally, for 10 minutes. You want the garlic to brown, not burn, so adjust the heat if necessary.

Meanwhile, in a medium nonplastic bowl, add the red pepper flakes, sugar, paprika, cayenne pepper, and salt, and stir to combine.

Place a fine-mesh strainer over the bowl and pour the garlic-oil mixture through the strainer into the bowl. Reserve the strained garlic. Stir the spices and oil mixture in the bowl until the sugar has dissolved, then add the sesame oil and stir to combine. When the spice-oil mixture has cooled, add the crisped garlic and stir. Serve immediately, or store in a covered container in the fridge for up to 6 months.

Super Simple Baked Fish

Serves 4

1 pound boneless, skinless halibut fillets

Olive oil for coating

Flaky sea salt and freshly ground black pepper

Juice from ½ large lemon

3 tablespoons salted butter

3 garlic cloves, coarsely minced

3 tablespoons coarsely chopped fresh flat-leaf parsley or chives

This is the easiest fish recipe around, taught to me by my friend Alli. It's incredible that a meal can be so quick and easy but delicious enough to wow a crowd. I especially love using halibut for this divine preparation. There are only a few ingredients, so it's key to use high-quality options (like Maldon salt and Kerrygold butter) and watch them come together and transform into something so satisfying.

Preheat the oven to 450°F.

Cut the halibut fillets into 5 to 6 evenly portioned pieces. Lightly coat the bottom of an 8 by 8-inch baking dish or 10-inch ovenproof skillet with olive oil and add the fish. Generously season the fish with salt and pepper. Generously coat each fillet in olive oil, then squeeze lemon juice over each piece. Top each piece of fish with a pat of butter and sprinkle with garlic and parsley. Bake until the fish flakes easily with a fork, about 12 minutes, then remove from the oven. Spoon the melted butter sauce from the baking dish over each fish piece. Serve immediately.

Fish Alternatives

Snapper
Cod
White seabass

Mom's Veggie Sandwich

Serves 1

2 slices multigrain bread
2 tablespoons mayonnaise
Flaky sea salt and freshly ground black pepper
½ head green-leaf lettuce (6 to 8 leaves)
4 slices tomato
1 thin slice yellow onion
1 mini cucumber, thinly sliced
Enough thick-sliced sharp Cheddar cheese for a single layer
Sliced avocado (optional)

A veggie sandwich might seem too simple to belong in a cookbook, but I don't care. This was a sandwich my mom used to make me, and it just hits a spot on my deliciousness meter that will leave me craving it until the day I die. How can simple raw veggies and cheese in between bread be so satisfying? Well, first of all, it's not bread, it's toast, and getting each slice brown and brickle really makes for a great texture contrast. The amounts of the ingredients listed are approximations, but be sure to be generous with flaky salt and black pepper. Don't skimp on the mayo, either! Of course, this is easy to scale up for more people—it's a sandwich!

In the toaster, toast the bread until golden brown. Spread mayonnaise on one side of both slices of toasted bread, making sure the mayonnaise layer evenly covers the entire surface. Every bite must have mayonnaise—this is important. Sprinkle salt and pepper on top of the mayonnaise on both slices of bread (I like a generous amount of both). On one piece of bread, layer the lettuce, tomato, and onion, and top with another light grinding of pepper and light sprinkle of salt. Then overlap the cucumber, cheese, and avocado (if using). Close the sandwich with the second bread slice, mayo-side down, and slice in half.

Nature Thrives in Diversity

People sometimes have strong reactions toward me spearing fish or bowhunting for deer. Rather than take offense, I find it fascinating to explore the reasons why. Modern society has raised us to not think about where our food comes from. Most of what's sold to consumers has been industrialized, cut, reshaped, packaged, processed, and renamed until we no longer recognize it as a being that once lived. We've come to understand the word *civilized* as valuing the distance we've developed between ourselves and our most basic necessities of survival, and it can be considered "savage" to take a life to feed ourselves, or to gut and clean a harvest with our own two hands. If "civilized" simply means being as disconnected from the source of our necessities as possible, then I'll proudly stay on team "savage" forever.

Nature doesn't naturally grow as a uniform line of monocrops identical in shapes and sizes. Nature thrives in diversity. It's the biodiversity that adds richness to the soil and life to the reefs and harmony to the overall picture. Here's the thing—we ARE nature. We are not separate from it. And it's our individually unique, beautiful diversity that is going to add communal harmony to this wonderful world. And that's why it's great that we make different choices, based on where we live and who we are.

If globally, we all target the same species of fish, their population will collapse and the whole ocean suffers. Eating locally abundant species, especially if they are less popular and lower on the food chain, can help restore balance. So can learning to use the whole animal. One deer, one cow, even one chicken can stretch so far if we embrace every edible part. It's not just about yield—it's about honoring the animal, tasting more flavors, and receiving the full nutritional benefit.

By sharing stories of truth and connection about food, we all can decide for ourselves how to curate our own paths. Want to go vegan? Great! I hope you can find ways to examine your meals and the practices that brought them to your plate. Don't want to eat octopus because you saw a movie and just can't do it? Cool, more for me. And I'm not being facetious; I say that with love. I sincerely support peoples' personal choices of what they put into their bodies. The more unique our footprints are, the better. With so many humans on this planet, diversity isn't just beautiful—it's essential.

Ginger Coconut Poke

Serves 4 to 6 as an appetizer

1½ pounds boneless, skinless aku fillet (skipjack tuna), cut into ½-inch cubes

¼ cup Ginger Sesame Sauce (page 40), chilled

¾ cup unsweetened full-fat coconut milk

2 tablespoons freshly squeezed lime juice

2 teaspoons flaky sea salt

Fish Alternatives

Snapper
Ono (wahoo)
Trevally

This recipe came together by happy accident. I brought a jar of green ginger sauce on a dive trip, expecting to spear a nice goatfish to steam up. Instead, I got an aku (skipjack tuna), which I normally eat raw as sashimi. I cubed it into poke and added some of the green sauce. I also had a fresh coconut on hand and some limes, so I grated the coconut and made milk and mixed it with some lime juice and holy moly, was it jamming! The ginger and sesame notes, mixing with creamy, sweet coconut, work so beautifully in a delightfully unexpected way!

In a medium bowl, combine the fish, ginger sesame sauce, coconut milk, lime juice, and salt. Stir, then taste and adjust the seasoning. Serve immediately.

Aku

Aku (skipjack tuna) is a beloved fish in Hawai'i, but it is often snubbed, thrown back, or just used for bait on the mainland. Many people eat aku all the time without realizing it as it's the most common tuna found in cans or pouches on the shelves of grocery stores. But fresh aku is such a beautiful delicacy. The meat is a gorgeous ruby red and so soft. Aku don't get as big as the more popular tuna species, but they do get even tastier as they grow.

Fresh aku has to be treated well. It should be iced or refrigerated immediately and fillets wrapped in paper towels that should be changed daily. Without proper care, the soft meat can deteriorate faster than most. As long as you treat it like the gold it is, I can promise you that it will be an absolute hit as sashimi, tataki, carpaccio, sushi, or poke. I always fry up the bones right away and eat the meat off them. If I cook the fillets, I'll turn them into delicious fresh tuna sandwiches.

Aku is such a great food source since it is considered to be one of the most resilient and sustainable tuna species. It's also low in mercury and amazingly high in the powerful antioxidant selenium. So next time you catch an aku or have the chance to buy one, don't pass it up since it's definitely a fish that deserves more flowers than it receives.

Shrimp Truck–Style Garlic Fish

Serves 2 to 4

1 pound boneless, skinless mahimahi, cut into 8 pieces

Flaky sea salt

1½ tablespoons paprika

¼ cup olive oil

3 tablespoons salted butter

Cloves from 1 head of garlic, finely chopped

Juice of ½ lemon

Chopped fresh flat-leaf parsley for garnishing

Cooked white rice for serving

This is my fish riff on all the garlic shrimp trucks scattered across the North Shore of O'ahu. The tangy, buttery goodness with crispy garlic and paprika makes each bite explode with layers of flavors and crunch. It's easy to make, yet feels fancy enough for fine dining.

Season the mahimahi with salt and paprika, turning the fish pieces to coat them evenly.

In a large skillet over medium-high heat, warm the olive oil and butter. When the butter is bubbling, place the fish in a single layer in the skillet, leaving room between the pieces and working in batches if necessary. Cook until the fish begins to brown, about 2 minutes, and then flip to repeat on the other side. Transfer the fish from the skillet to a plate or a cutting board. Turn down the heat to medium-low, add the garlic, and stir. Once the garlic begins to slightly brown, about 1½ minutes, turn the heat off and add the lemon juice. Stir to combine, then spoon the sauce over the fish and garnish with parsley. Serve immediately over rice.

Fish Alternatives

Striped marlin
Cod
Halibut

Citrusy Grilled Fish

Serves 4

1½ pounds boneless, skinless grouper fillets

¾ cup olive oil

⅔ cup roughly chopped Thai basil or whatever fresh herbs you choose

½ cup shoyu

¼ cup freshly squeezed lemon juice

4 garlic cloves, roughly chopped

Freshly ground black pepper

This six-ingredient marinade is bright and fragrant, allowing the essence of the fish to shine. But what I love most about this delicious meal is how easy and fast it is to make. It's a simple, yet staple recipe that I have given to friends from all over the world. I still get texts from people who make it over and over again. I often use Thai basil because it's what I grow and almost always have on hand, but you can use whatever fresh herbs you have available. The herbs you choose will be your flavor profile.

Cut the fish into 4 to 6 portions. In a medium mixing bowl, combine the olive oil, basil, shoyu, lemon juice, garlic, and pepper, and stir briefly. Place the fish pieces in the bowl and fully submerge them in the liquid. Cover and store in the fridge for at least 30 minutes or up to 2 hours.

Preheat a grill to high heat (450°F).

Remove the fish from the marinade, shake gently, and place on the grill. Cook without moving the fish for 3 to 5 minutes, then flip and grill on the other side until the fish is cooked all the way through (you should be able to cut through it easily with a fork), another 3 to 5 minutes. This is fast, high-heat grilling, so you want to monitor the fish to make sure it doesn't burn. If it begins to cook too fast, move the fish to a cooler part of the grill. Serve immediately.

Fish Alternatives

White seabass
'Ahi
Mahimahi

Venison Patty Melt

Serves 1

⅓ pound ground venison or beef
Flaky sea salt
2 thin slices yellow onion, cut into 2-inch pieces
Olive oil for sautéing
Freshly ground black pepper
Mayonnaise
2 slices bread (sourdough or multigrain)
Enough sharp white Cheddar cheese to cover the burger
Salted butter for sautéing

Toppings
Ketchup
Mustard
Thinly sliced dill pickle
3 slices tomato
1 lettuce leaf

If you love simple cheeseburgers like I do, this one's for you. It's the pure foundation of a classic burger with no bells and whistles. I use bread, not buns, because that's what I usually have on hand without having to go to the store. And browning the bread in the pan right before serving takes it to another level. I like to serve this with crisped up 'Ulu Tots (page 122) if I have some in my freezer.

On a piece of parchment paper bigger than your bread slice, use a spatula to press the ground venison into a patty ⅓ inch high. Season the top with salt. Cover the meat with half of the onion, and gently press it in.

In a medium skillet over medium-high heat, add enough olive oil to coat the bottom of the skillet, and warm the oil. Place the patty into the pan onion-side down, keeping the parchment paper on. If the patty has lost its shape, use the spatula to shape the patty again while it's cooking. Place a meat press or some type of weight (a small pan will do) on top of the parchment-covered patty. Cook until charred, about 4 minutes, peel off the parchment paper, season the top with salt and pepper, and then flip the patty. Add more oil if necessary and cook for 1 minute on the other side, gently pressing with the spatula. Transfer the patty to a plate and scoop out any remaining onion bits from the pan.

Smear a layer of mayonnaise onto both slices of bread. Place the venison patty over the mayonnaise on one slice, then cover it with Cheddar cheese and top with the other slice of bread, mayonnaise-side in.

Wipe the skillet clean, and place it on the stove over medium-high heat. When the skillet is hot, melt enough butter to coat the bottom of the skillet. Place the burger (bread and all) in the skillet and cook. Use your meat press to hold the burger down (or press it firmly with the spatula). When the bread is golden brown, 2 to 3 minutes, flip the burger and add more butter to the skillet. When both sides of the bread are brown, transfer the burger to a plate. On the side without the cheese, lift the bread and add the ketchup, mustard, pickle, tomato, lettuce, and remaining half of the onion on the burger. I like to add another light hit of salt and pepper, then close up the burger. Serve immediately.

FREE
FLY

7

Backyard Gatherings

Feasts for a Crowd

I remember it clearly. I was in the Arctic Circle during the freezing dark of winter and had just gone diving with orcas. More than the great white shark in Mexico or the sperm whales in Dominica, this interaction was one that I anticipated with anxiety. As a kid, I'd had recurring dreams about orcas. They were always happy and peaceful dreams, but as I grew older, the thought of swimming with them both intrigued and frightened me. I started to wonder if that's how I would die. It might sound silly, but that's the truth.

Spoiler alert: I didn't die, and it was absolutely thrilling—I actually ended up in the middle of a pod while they were hunting! But when I got back on the boat and warmed up with a glass of whiskey, I heard my inner voice say, "I'm good now. I can be done. We did it. Let's go home." I had never felt that before. I had started to wonder if I'd just live the rest of my life on the road as long as the opportunities kept coming. But that voice stuck with me. And in the trips that came and went after that one, I found myself a little less present—wondering what the winds were doing in Hawaiʻi, whether the seas were calm, or if there were mangoes on the trees. I found myself yearning to have not just a home base, but a real home. And sometimes things happen fast when you set an intention.

Soon after this realization, Justin and I were driving back to the house we were renting in a neighborhood we love when I saw someone putting up a for-sale sign on the corner of a nearby street. "Let's just go pretend!" I said, and we both agreed that we were simply nosy enough to pull over and ask the real estate agent for a spontaneous showing just so we could see the inside of the house. It was old, built in the 1950s, and had had only one owner, an elderly Japanese woman who had passed away. It was a simple house, but it had soul. When we walked into the humble and intimate backyard, hidden from the road and lined with a border of ti leaf plants, I fell in love. There was a fish frying shack in the backyard. It was just a few wooden posts with a patchwork of tin as a roof, but there was still an old, rusted wok and a stool just sitting in the middle. When I saw that old, rusty shack and thought of the memories it held and the people it had fed, my heart felt something.

Justin recognized the look in my eyes, and as we left, he reminded me that we were just playing pretend. But a month later, we were in escrow for that house, and right before it was time to get the keys, we found out that we were also pregnant. Like I said, life moves fast and when it did, we knew it was now time to go slow. We wanted to be here in our home and get ready to become a family. So rather than traveling the world for work, we brought our production skills home, and we started a YouTube channel about foraging, food, and family, cooking true-blue Hawaiʻi food right in our backyard. And oh, the gatherings and guests this backyard has held! Our home is a place where people stop by often. Fishermen stop in to share extra slabs of fish, and friends bring avocados and citrus in abundance. Most visitors leave with a meal in their belly or something in hand. It's not bartering though—there's never anything transactional about it. Our home is a place of sharing and a hub of love for the bounty of nature that surrounds us and for the appreciation of a real community. Dinners at our place are casual and rootsy, but we always have one formality—a simple gathering into a circle before our meal to say thanks to one another and to the plants and animals that feed us, while sharing the stories of the food to come. It feels quite full circle to me, especially after years of travel, to return home to a simple life of living close to nature and taking care of that which cares for us, just like my parents did.

Italian-Style Fish Carpaccio

Serves 4 to 6 as an appetizer

1 pound boneless, skinless ono (wahoo) fillet or any medium to large fish that you can eat raw (see page 20)

1 teaspoon flaky sea salt

¼ teaspoon freshly ground black pepper

1 teaspoon caper brine

2 tablespoons capers

1 tablespoon minced red onion

1 tablespoon chopped fresh flat-leaf parsley or cilantro

⅓ cup olive oil

3 tablespoons freshly squeezed lemon or lime juice

This is my go-to dish to bring to a gathering. It's sophisticated, scrumptious, and takes only a few ingredients, making it a fast, yet fancy way to impress a crowd. There are layers of happiness in this simple dish—bright notes of citrus, briny punches of capers, and the fresh textures and flavors of raw herbs and onions—all wrapped up in good-quality olive oil for pure, silky bliss! I realized how often I make this dish for parties when one night I instead brought a beautiful platter of pure and simple sashimi, and the crowd oohed and aahed over the presentation. Buddy squeezed his way through everyone to peek up and see the plate of beautifully arranged raw fish, only to shout with extreme disappointment, "Mommmmm!!! You forgot all the green stuff!!" Needless to say, Buddy loves carpaccio!

Using a sharp knife, slice the fish fillet into long rectangles roughly 1¼ inches high by 3 inches wide. Then cut the fish into slices ¼ inch thick. Overlap the slices on a serving plate, exposing the majority of each piece's surface area. Season with salt and pepper.

Evenly splash the caper brine over the fish. Top with the capers, onion, and parsley. Drizzle the olive oil over the fish. Finish with the lemon juice and slightly tilt the plate around to more evenly distribute the liquids. The most important part is to get every piece of fish evenly seasoned with all the toppings. Serve immediately.

Do Ahead: *If I'm bringing this to a party, I like to prepare the dish up to the point of drizzling the olive oil, then refrigerate until serving, and then add the oil and lemon juice just before serving.*

Fish Alternatives

Snapper
Yellowtail
'Ahi

Nigiri Sushi

Serves 4 to 6

⅓ cup rice vinegar

2 tablespoons cane sugar

Fine sea salt

2 cups sushi or Calrose white rice

2½ cups water

Wasabi for serving (optional)

1½ pounds sashimi-grade boneless, skinless 'ahi (yellowfin tuna) fillet or any fish you can eat raw (see page 20)

1 lemon, scrubbed and cut into extremely thin slices, then halved (optional)

Pickled ginger for serving (optional)

Shoyu for dipping

Raw fish and cooked rice. At first I wondered if this is too simple to be worthy of a published recipe. But nigiri sushi is something special, highly sought-after and served in expensive restaurants but rarely made at home. And I think it can be intimidating to get it right because it is so wonderful and pure. From cooking the rice perfectly and seasoning with the right ratios of vinegar and sugar to choosing a quality cut of raw fish, nigiri is such a special treat to serve up.

In a small mixing bowl, combine the vinegar, sugar, and 1 teaspoon of salt. Stir briefly, then set aside to let the sugar dissolve.

Add the rice to a medium pot and rinse under cold running water, using your hands to stir and massage the rice until the water turns cloudy, then drain. Repeat the process. Add the 2½ cups of water to the pot with the rinsed rice. Bring to a simmer over medium heat, cover, and turn down the heat to as low as possible. Let the rice cook for 16 minutes, then turn the heat off and let sit for 5 minutes, keeping it covered. Pour the vinegar mixture over the rice and toss to evenly distribute.

In a medium bowl, combine 1½ cups of room-temperature water and 1 teaspoon of salt. When the rice is cool enough to handle but still warm, dip your hands in the water, then scoop out a ball of rice, 1½ to 2 tablespoons. Squeeze and mold the rice into a torpedo shape that is roughly 2 inches long with tapered ends. Set aside on a tray or a plate. Repeat the process until the rice is used up, dipping your hands in the water as needed (I find every other time works well), so the rice doesn't stick.

Spread a smudge of wasabi on each rice ball, if using.

Using a sharp knife, slice the fish fillet into long rectangles roughly 1¼ inches high by 3 inches wide. Then cut the fish into nigiri-size pieces ¼ inch thick. Let the fish slices fall on top of one another.

To assemble the nigiri, take one piece of fish and lay it like a blanket over a rice ball (I like to shape the edges of the fish around the rice). Lay a lemon slice on top of the nigiri, if using (I find it elevates the nigiri). Arrange the nigiri on a platter and repeat with the remaining fish and rice.

Serve with wasabi (if using), pickled ginger (if using), and shoyu on the side. I tell my guests to dip the nigiri in the shoyu fish-side down.

Fish Alternatives

Ono (wahoo)
Salmon
White seabass

Leftovers Charcuterie Board

Serves 8

Cured and Smoked Fish (page 97), sliced thinly
Cured and Smoked Venison (page 97), sliced thinly
Smoked Fish Dip (page 223)
Italian-Style Fish Carpaccio (page 211)
Spicy Poke (page 219)
Kimi's Kimchi (page 83)
Halved grape or cherry tomatoes
Torn butter lettuce
Thinly sliced red onion
Thinly sliced cucumber
Thinly sliced lemon
Pickled ginger
Pickled veggies of your choice
Fresh basil leaves or flat-leaf parsley
Olive oil for drizzling
Flaky sea salt and freshly ground black pepper
Capers and their brine
Sour cream
Crunchy Garlic Chili Oil (page 191)
Variety of sliced, toasted sourdough bread, baguette, and crackers (like multigrain and salted flatbread crackers) for serving

When I'm attending a gathering that I don't have time to cook for, a charcuterie board is my savior. I try to keep my fridge well stocked with cured, smoked fish and meat as well as a variety of pickled goods. Arranging these items with fresh veggies and crackers makes such a beautiful and gourmet board of snacks that are always appreciated. The list of ingredients below is a very loose guideline. When I make it, the ingredients change every single time. That's the whole point of a leftover board—use what you have!

On a large cutting board or platter, arrange the smoked fish, smoked venison, fish dip, carpaccio, poke, kimchi, tomato, lettuce, onion, cucumber, lemon, pickled ginger, pickled veggies, and basil. Drizzle olive oil over the tomato and lettuce, and season with salt and pepper. Put the capers and sour cream in small bowls, add a spoonful or two of the chili oil to the sour cream, then place on the cutting board, along with the bread and crackers. Add a variety of small knives and forks, and serve.

Grilled Fish Collars

Serves 6 to 8 as an appetizer

¾ cup shoyu

Juice from ½ lemon

2 teaspoons granulated sugar

2 tablespoons chopped green onions, white and green parts

6 skin-on fish collars (⅓ to ½ pound each) from 4- to 5-pound snappers (see Note)

Olive oil for drizzling

Flaky sea salt and freshly ground black pepper

Note: *Many Asian grocery stores sell fish collars. But if you're working with a whole fish, follow the fish fillet guide (see page 245) up to step 5 of the "Filleting" section. Then use kitchen shears or cleavers to cut the collars free from the head.*

Fish collars are throw-away cuts in the fish industry, but many fishermen consider the collar to be one of the tastiest pieces. Collars aren't as popular as fillets because you can't make them into a boneless piece of anything—you have to pick the meat out of the bone structure. But the different pockets and components formed by the bone structure help steam the meat to keep it juicy. Collar meat is some of the most flavorful and succulent. If you're willing to work for this meat, it's one of the most rewarding cuts. I like serving fish collars with a quick ponzu-style sauce that gets drizzled on right after they come off the grill.

Preheat a gas, charcoal, or wood grill to 450°F.

In a small bowl, mix the shoyu, lemon juice, and sugar, and stir until the sugar dissolves. Stir in the green onions and reserve.

Drizzle the olive oil over the fish collars. Season with salt and pepper. When the grill is ready, place the collars skin-side down on the grates, close the lid if your grill has a cover, and cook until golden brown, 5 to 6 minutes. Then flip and repeat on the other side. Transfer to a serving platter and drizzle the collars with the entire amount of the reserved shoyu mixture. Serve immediately.

Fish Alternatives

Yellowtail
Salmon
White seabass

Spicy Poke

Serves 4

1 pound ono (wahoo), diced small or minced

3 tablespoons diced white onion

2 to 3 green onions, white and green parts, sliced, plus more for garnishing

3 tablespoons mayonnaise

3 tablespoons toasted sesame oil

3 tablespoons tobiko

3 tablespoons Sriracha sauce

1 tablespoon chili oil

2 teaspoons flaky sea salt

White sesame seeds for garnishing (optional)

The key to a good spicy poke is balancing the mayo with touches of sesame and chili oil. This makes the poke extra silky and full of flavor. Spicy poke can be eaten as is, used as a dip for crackers, a spread, or a filling for sushi (see page 220). The small cuts also make this recipe an absolute winner for using every morsel of fish meat available. Odd pieces that are too small or irregularly shaped to cut into sashimi can be easily minced for spicy poke. After filleting fish, I often use a spoon to scrape any bits of meat left on the bones to make this crowd-pleasing favorite.

In a medium bowl, add the ono, white onion, green onions, mayonnaise, sesame oil, tobiko, Sriracha sauce, chili oil, and salt. Stir to combine thoroughly, then taste and adjust the seasoning. Scoop the poke into a medium serving bowl. Garnish with the green onions and sesame seeds (if using) and serve fresh immediately, or cover and chill in the fridge for 1 hour to let the flavors mingle.

Do Ahead: *The poke can be made 1 day in advance, covered, and stored in the fridge.*

Fish Alternatives

'Ahi
White seabass
Yellowjack

Spicy Poke Roll

Makes six 8-inch rolls

⅓ cup rice vinegar
2 tablespoons cane sugar
1 teaspoon sea salt
2 cups sushi or Calrose white rice
2½ cups water
6 full sheets roasted nori (seaweed)
2 mini cucumbers or 1 Japanese cucumber, seeded and cut lengthwise into ¼-inch thick strips
1 ripe avocado, cut into thin slices
1 recipe Spicy Poke (page 219)

Note: *If you are making these to bring to a party, they'll be easier to transport if you make the rolls ahead of time and slice them on-site.*

Spicy poke rolls are a true crowd-pleaser. I love to add fresh cucumber for a nice crunch and avocado for extra creaminess. These are great to make ahead of time, chill, and then take to a party or potluck, where you can slice them on-site and serve on a platter.

In a small mixing bowl, combine the vinegar, sugar, and salt. Stir briefly, then set aside to let the sugar dissolve.

Add the rice to a medium pot and rinse under cold running water, using your hands to stir and massage the rice until the water turns cloudy, then drain. Repeat the process. Add the 2½ cups of water to the pot with the rinsed rice. Bring to a simmer over medium heat, cover, and turn down the heat to as low as possible. Let the rice cook for 16 minutes, then turn the heat off and let sit for 5 minutes, keeping it covered. Remove the cover, then pour the vinegar mixture over the rice, and toss to distribute evenly.

When the rice is cool enough to touch, assemble the sushi rolls. Fill a small bowl with water to dip your fingers, rice paddle, and knife in to prevent the rice from sticking, and set it aside. Place a nori sheet rough-side up horizontally on a cutting board or a sushi mat. Dip the rice paddle in water, then scoop 1 cup of rice onto the nori sheet. Spread the rice evenly over the nori, leaving the top quarter (about 1¾ inches) bare. Lay a single line of cucumber strips across the rice ½ inch from the bottom, then repeat with the avocado above the cucumber. Spread ⅓ cup of the poke mixture above the line of avocado. Using a sushi mat if you have one, lift the bottom edge of the nori and roll it up and over the ingredients. Continue to roll tightly, tucking the bottom edge in, until complete. Place the roll seal-side down and reserve.

Repeat until all the ingredients have been used, or you've made the desired number of rolls.

Wet a sharp knife in the water and use it to slice each roll into eight pieces, 1 inch wide. Serve immediately.

Smoked Fish Dip

Serves 4 to 6 people as an appetizer

2 cups finely chopped or flaked Island-Style Smoked Fish (page 138) or any boneless, skinless smoked fish

8 ounces cream cheese, at room temperature

¼ cup minced red onion

¼ cup finely diced dill pickle

¼ cup chopped chives, plus more for garnishing

1 rib celery, diced

3 tablespoons sour cream

3 tablespoons mayonnaise

Zest from 1 lemon, plus some for garnishing

2 tablespoons freshly squeezed lemon juice

2 tablespoons dried dill

Flaky sea salt and freshly ground black pepper

Note: *To make the dip as a sandwich spread, I like to use half the amount of cream cheese and twice the mayonnaise.*

Think of this as an elevated tuna-fish sandwich spread—that's a compliment because I love tuna fish sandwiches. (See the Note for how to make this into a sandwich spread.) There's so much going on here: the fluffy, creamy combo of cream cheese, sour cream, and mayonnaise; the zing of the dill and lemon zest; and the punch and texture of the onions and pickles. The layers of flavor and texture work in a harmonious way that keeps you coming back for more. Serve it with crackers or sturdy kettle chips at a pau hana party, or bring it on board for a boat snack.

In a large mixing bowl, add the smoked fish, cream cheese, onion, pickle, chives, celery, sour cream, mayonnaise, lemon zest, lemon juice, and dill. Stir until thoroughly combined. Season with salt and pepper and garnish with more chives and lemon zest. Serve chilled.

Fish Alternatives

Marlin
Salmon
Mackerel

Grilled Octopus with Chimichurri

Serves 4 to 6

One 2- to 3-pound previously frozen octopus, defrosted (see Note)

2 tablespoons coarse sea salt

2 tablespoons olive oil

Chimichurri

½ cup minced fresh flat-leaf parsley

½ cup minced fresh cilantro

½ cup minced red onion

2 garlic cloves, minced

2 tablespoons minced fresh oregano or 1 tablespoon dried oregano

1 tablespoon red pepper flakes, or more as needed

⅓ cup olive oil

3 tablespoons red wine vinegar

1 tablespoon flaky sea salt

Note: *If you have fresh octopus, gut it by pulling the head inside out and removing the innards. Freeze the octopus in a resealable bag or covered container for at least 4 days to tenderize it before defrosting.*

continued

My friend Justin Lee, who is one of the most talented bowhunters and spearfishers in existence, taught me this recipe and it blew my mind! Chimichurri sauce with grilled octopus is a combo made in heaven. The method of pressure cooking in an electric pressure cooker makes the octopus tender and juicy, and hitting it with some flames from the grill for a bit of char and flavor takes this recipe to the next level. This dish is zingy, bright, and will awaken your taste buds. The red hues of cooked octopus complemented by the vibrant green chimichurri sauce makes it as beautiful as it is delicious.

To prep the octopus: Place the defrosted octopus in a large mixing bowl and sprinkle with salt. Use your hands to vigorously squeeze, push, and press the entire octopus for 7 minutes—think of it as a deep tissue massage. At the thicker parts of the legs and head, apply pressure as you squeeze. Thoroughly rinse the octopus in cold running water. It will foam somewhat; keep rinsing until all the suds are gone and the water runs clear.

Place the cleaned octopus in the pot of an electric pressure cooker. Add 2 cups of water. Lock the lid into place and cook on high pressure for 12 minutes. Manually release the pressure. (Alternatively, cook the octopus on a stovetop: In a medium pot over medium-high heat, add the octopus and 3 cups of water. Bring to a boil, then turn down the heat to medium-low, cover, and let simmer for 1 hour.)

When the steam has released from the pressure cooker, remove the lid and pierce the thickest part of the octopus with a wooden chopstick or a fork to make sure it punctures easily. If the octopus is not done, put it back in the pressure cooker and cook on high pressure for another 2 minutes. Repeat if necessary. Using tongs, transfer the octopus from the pressure cooker and place it in a large mixing bowl. Drizzle with olive oil and reserve.

To make the chimichurri: In a medium bowl, add the parsley, cilantro, onion, garlic, oregano, and red pepper flakes, and mix until thoroughly combined. (For a more intense flavor, smash and grind the herbs and spices in a mortar and pestle first.) If you love chile flakes, go ahead and add more. Add the olive oil, vinegar, and salt, and stir to combine. Reserve.

To grill the octopus: Prepare a gas, charcoal, or wood grill to high heat (450°F). Place the octopus on the grate and cook until charred, 4 to 5 minutes, then flip and cook the other side until charred. Transfer the octopus to a cutting board.

Grilled Octopus with Chimichurri

continued

When the octopus is cool enough to touch, use a sharp knife to cut the head off above the eyes. Moving down 1½ inches, make another horizontal cut across the body below the eyes. Discard the section with the eyes. To remove the beak, flip the leg portion over to see the underside, and locate a small, hard black dot (the beak) in the center of the body. Make a deep incision from the beak toward a section where two legs meet, then open the flaps to reveal the whole beak. Using a paring knife, gently cut the beak from the body. Remove it and discard.

To serve: Thinly slice the head and the thickest part of the legs into bite-size portions. For the skinnier part of the legs, make the pieces longer, about 1 inch. Place the pieces on a deep-rimmed serving dish that can hold a sauce, then spoon the chimichurri over the warm octopus and serve immediately.

Do Ahead: *The octopus can be parcooked in the electric pressure cooker up to 2 days in advance and stored undressed in the fridge in a covered container.*

Pule

At any of my backyard gatherings, there will always be a moment where everyone forms a circle and holds hands as we take the time to describe the dishes we are about to eat—where they came from, who harvested them, and how they were prepared. I love asking anyone who contributed to the meal to talk about their harvest or contribution. Oftentimes fishing stories are shared or vegetables are praised. It's also at this time that we give thanks to one another and celebrate whatever occasion brought us together. It is a sacred circle formed the minute someone shouts "E pule kākou!" (Let us pray!). But you don't need to summon any particular god or end with "amen" if you don't want to. You do need to summon gratitude for all that we have and for the plants and animals that feed us. Although it's not a formality, it can sure feel like one when you are about to lead a pule, but just remember you don't have to be religious to gather and give thanks for food. It might feel attention-seeking, nerve-wracking, or even boastful to have others gather and listen to you talk. Do it anyway. It's not about you. It's about collectively appreciating the beautiful parts of nature that we put into our bodies. Giving thanks and real descriptions of the food and processes of preparing it is honoring the love woven into every bite. It makes the meal more meaningful, more intentional, and more special. Do not rush through it. Set the tone.

Fish Burgers

Serves 4

Olive oil for sautéing
½ yellow onion, minced
½ carrot, peeled and minced
2 garlic cloves, minced
1 pound boneless skinless grouper, or any kind of boneless, skinless fish pieces, finely minced
½ cup canned water chestnuts, drained and minced
3 green onions, white and green parts, minced
¼ cup fresh cilantro leaves, minced
1 egg
Flaky sea salt and freshly ground black pepper
Salted butter for sautéing
4 hamburger buns
Toppings: Tomato, avocado, yellow onion, lettuce (optional)
Condiments: Dill pickle relish, ketchup, stone-ground mustard, yellow mustard (optional)

Fish burgers are really satisfying because they are so meaty and hearty, yet they don't bog you down. What I especially love about making them is that you don't have to use sashimi-grade fish. Adding the medley of vegetables gives them this healthful feel and texture. They don't come across as "fishy"—just as a good patty of protein with fresh ingredients.

In a large skillet over medium-high heat, warm 1 teaspoon of olive oil. Add the onion and carrot and cook for 4 minutes, stirring occasionally. Then add the garlic and cook until the veggies soften, about 1 minute. Turn off the heat and reserve.

In a large bowl, add the onion mixture, fish, water chestnuts, green onions, cilantro, and egg. Season with 1 teaspoon each of salt and pepper and stir the mixture with a spoon. Divide the mixture into four portions and shape them into large patties on a baking sheet or cutting board.

Wipe the large skillet clean, add enough olive oil to coat the bottom of the skillet, and warm over medium-high heat. Once the oil is hot and shimmering, use a spatula to transfer the patties to the skillet. (You may need to do this in two batches.) Season the patties lightly with salt and pepper. Cook until they are browned on one side, 3 minutes, then flip and repeat on the other side. Transfer the cooked patties to a plate and repeat with the remaining patties if necessary.

Wipe the skillet and return it to the stove over medium-high heat. Add ½ tablespoon of butter to the skillet. When it has melted, toast the burger buns.

To serve, assemble the burgers with your choice of toppings and condiments. Serve immediately.

Fish Alternatives

Sheepshead
Palani (surgeonfish)
Tautog (blackfish)

Potatoes au Gratin

Serves 6 to 8

1 cup heavy cream

3 russet potatoes, very thinly sliced (about ⅛-inch thick)

Flaky sea salt and freshly ground black pepper

Nutmeg for seasoning

½ yellow onion, thinly sliced

4 garlic cloves, finely chopped

3 cups shredded white sharp Cheddar cheese

9 sprigs thyme, destemmed

3 tablespoons chopped fresh flat-leaf parsley, plus more for garnishing

This easy combination of potatoes drenched in heavy cream yields the most decadent, beautiful, savory dish. I tend to make it to serve a crowd—it's the perfect melty, crispy side for dishes like grilled venison (see page 115) and many other party dishes. I love the way it even looks pretty in its simplicity; the pattern the potatoes form when I lay them in the pan is just a glorious thing. I'd always use a knife to slice my potatoes as thin as possible because I didn't own a mandoline. But I recently borrowed one for this recipe, and I'm a convert.

Preheat the oven to 425°F.

In a 10-inch ovenproof skillet, coat the bottom of the skillet with ¼ cup of the heavy cream, using a spatula to spread the cream evenly. Starting at the outer perimeter of the pan, place a layer of potatoes over the cream, slightly overlapping the slices. Season with salt, pepper, and a light sprinkle of nutmeg. Sprinkle one-third of the onion and garlic over the potatoes. Evenly sprinkle 1 cup of the cheese over the top, followed by one-third of the thyme and chopped parsley, then drizzle ¼ cup of the heavy cream. Repeat the layering process twice for a total of three layers. Put the filled skillet in the oven and cook until the top is brown, about 1 hour. After 30 minutes, check on the potatoes by piercing them with a sharp knife. Repeat after another 15 minutes. If it's browning too quickly, cover loosely with aluminum foil. It's ready when you can easily pierce the potatoes with a sharp knife. Remove from the oven and let it cool slightly before serving. Garnish with the parsley.

patagonia

Beer-Battered Fish Sliders with Chunky Dill Pickle Sauce

Makes 6 to 8 sliders

1 pound boneless, skinless mahimahi fillet

Coarse sea salt

¾ cup all-purpose flour

3 tablespoons seafood spice blend (see Note)

Olive oil for frying

1 cup cold beer, plus more as needed (you will taste the beer flavor, so choose one that you like)

One 12-ounce package Hawaiian sweet bread rolls, or 9-ounce package slider buns

Salted butter for sautéing

Lettuce leaves for garnishing

Thinly sliced red onion for garnishing

Chunky Dill Pickle Sauce

1 cup chopped dill pickles

¾ cup mayonnaise

1 tablespoon dried dill

1 tablespoon freshly squeezed lemon juice

Freshly ground black pepper

Note: *I like to use seafood spice blends that contain red pepper, paprika, and garlic, but use whichever one you like best!*

Fish Alternatives

Lingcod
Halibut
Grouper

Good beer-battered fried fish is a glorious thing, and it's never more glorious than when it's served in between soft sweet bread with chunky dill pickle tartar sauce. I'm a little particular about beer-battered fish—I don't like it when there's more batter than fish. The secret is the spices, because they don't just add flavor, they also make the batter lighter and crispier when fried. It's also important to dredge the fish in the seasoned flour—don't skip this step. It's the glue that makes the batter stick to the fish. Make sure the flour looks "dirty" and that the color of the spices comes through before adding the beer. The batter should also be a tiny bit on the thinner side. As you coat each floured fish piece in the batter, the liquid will thicken up, so add more beer as you go if necessary.

With a sharp knife, cut the fish fillet into roughly 2 by 4 by 1-inch rectangular pieces. Season the pieces with salt on all sides.

Battering the fillets is a two-part process: In a medium bowl, mix the flour and seafood spice blend. Working with one piece of fish at a time, dredge the fish in the flour-spice mix, making sure to coat every side, and place them on a clean plate. Reserve the flour-spice mix.

Place a wire rack over a baking pan and set near the stove. In a large, heavy skillet over medium-high heat, warm ½ inch of olive oil.

While the oil is heating, slowly whisk 1 cup of the beer into the remaining flour-spice mixture until smooth. (I like the consistency of the batter to coat the back of a spoon.) If the mixture gets too thick as you dip the fish into the batter, add extra beer to adjust the consistency as needed.

Once the oil is hot and shimmering, submerge a piece of the dredged fish in the beer batter to completely coat it, then carefully add the battered fish to the skillet. Repeat the process with additional fish pieces until you have enough to fit in the pan in a single layer without touching one another.

Cook the fish until the bottoms are brown, about 4 minutes, then carefully flip each piece. Turn down the heat to medium. When the fish pieces are crispy with a rich brown crust on both sides, another 4 minutes, transfer them to the prepared wire rack to cool. Working in batches, fry the rest of the fish pieces, turning the heat back up to medium-high before each batch, and reserve.

To make the pickle sauce: Add the pickles, mayonnaise, dill, lemon juice, and pepper to a medium bowl. Mix thoroughly and reserve.

To assemble the sliders: Slice the bread rolls in half. In a skillet over medium-high heat, melt a pat of butter. Place the rolls in the skillet open-side down and toast until just browned, about 1 minute.

Assemble the sliders by stacking on top of one bun a heaping tablespoon of pickle sauce, a lettuce leaf, a piece of fish, some sliced red onion, and then another heaping tablespoon of pickle sauce before topping with the other bun. Repeat until you have six to eight sandwiches made. Serve immediately.

Sweet-and-Sour Fish

Serves 6 to 8

Neutral oil for frying

2 pounds whole snapper, gutted and scaled

Flaky sea salt

1 cup all-purpose flour

2 tablespoons toasted sesame oil

1 red, orange, or yellow bell pepper, sliced, then cut into 1-inch segments

½ yellow onion, sliced thinly, then cut into 1-inch pieces

One 3-inch knob fresh ginger, finely chopped

1 garlic clove, finely chopped

½ cup apple cider vinegar

½ cup water, plus 2 teaspoons

⅓ cup light brown sugar

¼ cup shoyu

¼ cup ketchup

2 teaspoons cornstarch

Chopped fresh cilantro for garnishing

I bought the book *365 Ways to Cook Chinese* when I was a teenager because I wanted to make Panda Express–type food for myself. I cooked so many recipes from that book and felt like I had the key to this secret world of Chinese fast food. One of my family's favorites was sweet-and-sour pork. Later in life when I started diving, my uncle Billy wanted to find a new way to make whole fish, aside from steamed. So, we fried a whole uhu (parrotfish), and I made an adaption of the sweet-and-sour sauce and poured it over the fish. It's still something he asks for today.

In a large skillet over medium-high heat, add ½ inch of neutral oil.

While the oil is heating, use a sharp knife to make diagonal slits on the fish from the gills to the tail, breaking the skin and cutting to the bone, then repeat in the other direction to make a crosshatch. Flip the fish over and repeat on the other side.

Hold the fish up so it bends, and season with salt, allowing the salt to slip into the incisions. Flip the fish over and repeat on the other side. If your fish is too long to fit whole in the skillet, cut it into halves or thirds.

Place a wire rack over a baking pan and set near the stove. Place the flour on a large plate. To check if the oil is hot enough, carefully dip the fish tail in the oil. If it bubbles, the oil is ready. When the oil is hot enough, dredge the fish in the flour, making sure it's evenly coated on all sides, then carefully add it to the pan. Turn down the heat to medium and cook until golden brown, 5 to 7 minutes, then flip and repeat on the other side. Using tongs, transfer the fish to the prepared wire rack to cool.

In a small saucepan over medium-high heat, warm the sesame oil. Add the bell pepper and onion and cook, stirring occasionally. After 1 minute, stir in the ginger and garlic and continue to cook. After 1 minute, stir in the apple cider vinegar, ½ cup of the water, the brown sugar, shoyu, and ketchup. Bring to a boil, then turn down the heat to medium-low.

In a small bowl, mix the cornstarch with the remaining 2 teaspoons of water. Whisk the cornstarch mixture into the vinegar mixture and simmer until thickened, about 5 minutes.

Arrange the fried fish (or the pieces back into a whole form) on a platter. Pour the sauce over the fish, then garnish with cilantro and serve.

Fish Alternatives

Uhu (parrotfish)
Grouper
Calico bass

Greek-Style Pita Wraps with Venison Meatballs

Serves 6 to 8

Salad

1½ cups diced mini or Japanese cucumbers

1½ cups diced cherry tomatoes

1 cup diced red onion

2 tablespoons minced fresh oregano

Flaky sea salt and freshly ground black pepper

1 cup crumbled feta cheese

1 orange or red bell pepper, diced

1 cup kalamata or black olives

⅓ cup olive oil

2 tablespoons red wine vinegar

Juice of ½ lemon

Venison Meatballs

1½ pounds ground venison or lean ground beef

One 6-ounce can black olives, drained, rinsed, and roughly chopped

¾ cup finely diced red onion

¾ cup chopped fresh cilantro

¾ cup chopped fresh flat-leaf parsley

¾ cup chopped fresh mint

⅓ cup chopped fresh oregano

6 garlic cloves, minced

1 tablespoon dried dill

1 teaspoon flaky sea salt

½ teaspoon freshly ground black pepper

4 eggs

2 slices bread, torn into ½-inch pieces

1 cup crumbled feta cheese

Olive oil for frying

Olive oil for sautéing

12 slices of pita

One 16-ounce container hummus

One 16-ounce container tzatziki

These meatballs will knock your socks off. The mixture of ground meat, vegetables and herbs, feta cheese, and olives is such perfection. But their full potential is realized in these pita wraps covered in creamy hummus, tangy tzatziki, and crunchy salad. Sometimes I like to smash the meatballs into patties because they cook faster and you can fit more in a pita.

To make the salad: In a large bowl, add the cucumbers, tomatoes, onion, and oregano. Season with salt and pepper and stir. Add the feta cheese, bell pepper, and olives. Drizzle with olive oil, vinegar, and lemon juice. Toss well, cover, and reserve.

To make the meatballs: In a large mixing bowl, add the venison, olives, onion, cilantro, parsley, mint, oregano, garlic, and dill. Season with salt and pepper. Crack the eggs into the mixture and stir until well combined. Add the bread pieces to the mixture and stir to combine. Gently fold in the feta cheese. Using your hands, use about 2 tablespoons of the meat mixture to form each meatball.

Place a platter near the stove. In a large skillet over medium heat, warm ¼ inch of olive oil. Working in batches, carefully place the meatballs in the pan, leaving enough room so they do not touch one another. When the meatballs have started to nicely brown, about 3 minutes, gently flip them. Continue to turn the meatballs every 3 minutes until they are evenly brown on all sides, about 15 minutes total. Transfer them to the platter to cool. Repeat with the rest of the meatballs, adding more oil to the skillet as necessary.

To toast the pitas: In a large skillet over medium-high heat, add enough olive oil to coat the bottom of the skillet, and warm the oil. One at a time, add a pita to the skillet and toast on both sides until brown, about 30 seconds on each side. Repeat for the remaining pitas. Stack them on a plate for assembly.

To serve: Set up a pita bar with a stack of toasted pitas, meatballs, salad, hummus, and tzatziki, with all the elements lined up separately to let people make their own wrap.

How to Scale, Gut, Fillet, and Store Fish

Most people using this book will likely be buying fish already prepped from stores, but in case any of you are curious or have the opportunity to catch and clean your own fish, this is for you. (I have a fish cleaning and cutting 101 video on my YouTube channel that might be helpful too.) To me, there's no better feeling than fetching ingredients straight from the source and seeing them through by turning them into a meal with my own two hands.

The number-one rule of filleting a fish: It's okay if you mess up. Give yourself grace—there's always something that you can do to fix it, and perfect cuts come with practice. If you follow this basic information, it will be good enough and it will be delicious.

A few helpful tips:

- If you can, fillet your fish at a table that is tall enough so that you don't have to bend over. This will save your back.
- Before I cut fish, I make sure my knife is sharp. I keep honing my blade if I feel the knife getting dull throughout the process. Having a sharp knife will not only make the whole process easier, but it will also allow you to make cleaner cuts. There is a whole world of information about sharpening and honing knives out there; YouTube is your friend.
- Scaling and gutting fish can be a messy process that I prefer to do outside!
- After filleting, I bury my fish frames and guts in the garden.

Fish Scaling

I almost always scale my fish unless it's a big pelagic fish (those that live in the upper layers of the open sea, like ʻahi or mahimahi). Technically, you don't need to if you're removing the skin—but it is a good idea to at least scale where you're going to cut so that your knife enters the skin more easily, and scales don't get into the meat. I use a fish scaler, but if you don't have one, the edge of a metal spoon works great.

Place your fish on a surface that you can easily rinse clean. Place the scaler prong-side down on your fish. Put your other hand on the head of the fish to hold it steady. Think of it as an itchy fish; begin to scratch it against the grain, making sure to also scale the cheeks of the fish as well as underneath the fins. You are doing it right if the scales are flying off. Flip the fish over and scale the other side. After you are confident all the scales are removed, rinse and wash your cleaning area and the fish, making sure to pat the fish dry before filleting.

Gutting

1. Poke the tip of the knife into the anal hole (the small hole next to the underside fin closest to the tail) and cut toward the head, going around the pelvic fins (the pair of fins on the underside closest to the head); this helps you avoid needing to saw through bones. Once you're past the pelvic fins, continue on toward the head until you split open where the body meets the jaw, sawing through any tension that you feel.

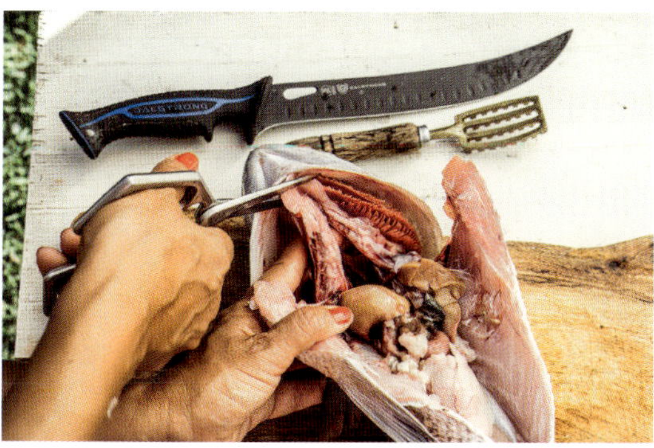

2. Use your hands to spread the flaps below the jaw open like a butterfly. If you can't do this with your hands, use a knife instead. Once both flaps are open, grip and pull the gills to remove them. Gills are connected at two points: One point comes right into the chin of the fish, and the other is connected inside against the back of the head. Break both of these connections to the chin by gripping and pulling the gills (for bigger, tougher fish, you may need to use your knife or kitchen shears). All the guts should come out with the gills. Rinse the fish and the cutting board.

Filleting

1. Place the whole fish on a cutting board horizontally with the back ridge of the fish closest to you. Insert your knife behind the head and cut along the back ridge to the tail in one clean sweep. Reinsert your knife and repeat this same cut, moving in toward the fish's spine to separate the fillet from the bones, until you reach the fish spine. Use the bones to guide your knife. You can lift the fillet off the bones as you cut it to see better.

2. At the smallest part of the fillet next to the tail, push the tip of your knife over the spine and puncture through the skin on the other side. Guide your blade toward the tail until the small flap releases.

continued

Filleting continued

3. Reposition the fish so that the belly section is closest to you. Starting at that small flap, insert your knife and cut from the tail to the gut cavity. Repeat this cut, moving in toward the spine until the back half of the fillet is released. As the fillet releases, you can lift it up with your other hand to help you see what you're doing.

4. Use kitchen shears or a sharp knife to cut the rib bones that keep the fillet attached to the spine.

5. To release the fillet completely, make a diagonal cut from the head to behind the pectoral fin to the belly. Use kitchen shears to release the fillet if necessary.

Repeat the process on the other side of the fish. The fish head, bones, and collars can all be reserved for using in other recipes.

Skinning the Fillet

Lay the fillet skin-side down. Starting at the tail end, insert your knife between the skin and the meat. Using your free hand to grip the skin, cut away from yourself until the skinless fillet is released. Repeat for the other fillet. Use your knife to remove any spots of skin you might have missed.

Removing the Bones

1. Place one of the skinned fish fillets on a cutting board. Cut along the center line to separate the fillet that doesn't have rib bones.

2. Cut along the other side of the center line to remove it completely.

3. Insert your knife horizontally just below the rib bones. Cut away from yourself to remove the rib bones.

Repeat the process on the other half of the fish. Check if any of the bloodline (a dark red streak) is left on the fillet. If so, cut it out with your knife and discard.

Storing Fish

The best way to store your cleaned fish is to wrap it in a paper towel and place it in a resealable bag or an airtight food-storage container. It can be stored in the fridge for up to 1 week, but just make sure to change your paper towel every 1 or 2 days. The paper towel absorbs moisture, and moisture is what makes fish fishy, so you want to keep your fish as dry as possible while storing it.

To store the fish for longer, I suggest vacuum sealing and freezing. Vacuum-sealed fish can be stored for up to 1 year in the freezer.

The Making of *Kimi's Kitchen*

The making of this book took over our lives and my home for more than two years. Every photo you see is a real meal I cooked in my kitchen for our tiny but mighty team. No food stylists or big production—just a few friends wearing many hats, showing up day after day to make this book come true. Creating this way let us experience the generosity of our community: fishermen dropping off fresh catches, Buddy and Carly (our family assistant) running to the neighbor's yard to pick mangoes, and everyone pulling up a seat to taste what we're cooking. We got to create from the heart of the well-functioning ecosystem we were writing about, and it's what makes this book so special. It simply could not have been done in this manner if I didn't have the most talented, down-to-earth, multifaceted team in my corner.

The Team

Nicole Gormley—Co-Author and Photographer

It's not every day that an award-winning documentary director calls to say she'll put her filmmaking career on hold to move to Hawai'i to write a book with me. But I'm sure glad I answered that call. Nicole and I have collaborated on several different films throughout our friendship, and working with her is a dream. Her creative vision and the magic she makes in meaningful storytelling are such rare gifts and always an honor to be a part of. Throughout the making of this book, I got to watch her grow—not just as a cook—but as a spearfisher woman, learning to provide beautiful catches for herself and her own community.

Jenny Fiedler—Co-Author

Jenny is the only one on our team with any book experience, so thank goodness she has enough of it to carry us all. Her writing and cooking skills (she has a degree in English from Yale and a culinary degree—though she'd never tell anyone), combined with her unwavering support and confidence in this project, were the spine that kept these pages bound together. Jenny is our secret weapon—a quiet storm of brains, talent, and hilariously witty humor that makes every single day brighter.

Justin Turkowski—Photographer

My husband Justin has the true soul of a cameraman. He's humble and tries to stay out of the spotlight as much as possible, but his work in both photography and filmmaking speaks for itself. He received the Critics' Choice Documentary Award for Best Cinematography and was the creator of our cooking YouTube channel. There are endless ways this book wouldn't have existed without him—from covering for me as a partner and parent when I was buried in work, to stepping up so strongly when we needed his creative help. But mainly, for being my muse—because he cares about the values written here just as much as I do. The life we created together not only gave me my "Haiku" back but also cultivated the making of this book.

Carly Zech—Our Family Assistant

Carly is a young powerhouse who came into my life and made it so much better. I don't know many people who can keep up with the spontaneity of our work, family, and the adventures we pursue, but like a tree in the wind, Carly is as flexible as she is strong and rooted. From washing dishes, getting groceries, wrangling Buddy, cleaning fish, taking notes, and putting our home back together every day after it was hit by a culinary tornado—what an absolute force!

YETI

Mahalo

Mom, thank you for putting so much love into the meals you made us and for always encouraging me in the kitchen. Dad, thank you for taking me spearfishing. I didn't realize what a rare gift that was for a father to give his daughter.

Christy, I will never understand your endless capacity to give to others, but I do know how lucky I am to be a main receiver of your abundant support. Thank you for reading drafts, testing recipes, giving input, and for leaving your comfort zone to be in photos with me. I love you.

Randy, thanks for being the best fish nerd big brother a spearfishing little sister could ever ask for and for sharing your knowledge for the book. And thank you, Bubba!

To my editor, Kelly Snowden, for reaching out many years ago and planting the seed of this book. Thank you for being so patient year after year when I did nothing with that seed. And thank you to the team at Ten Speed Press (Emma Campion, Gabby Ureña Matos, and everyone else) who worked tirelessly to make this the best book it could be.

To Katie Finch, for believing in this project when it was still a dream. And Chris Ying, for the guidance before we knew what we were getting into.

To my literary agent, Tess Callero, for all your guidance and support. And my manager Blair Marlin, for putting so much work on hold so I could do this book.

Perrin James, DJ Struntz, Christa Funk, Ben Ono, Ryan McInnis, Nainoa Langer, Nani Welch, Asia Brynne, Mark Kushimi, Jody MacDonald—to simply thank you for the "additional photography" would be an understatement. Thank you for being the adventurers, travel partners, and friends who have documented so many of my life's favorite moments in your stunning photography. And thank you, Madeleine Rosenthal, for your photo assisting help behind the scenes.

To all our friends who helped with photo shoots and tested recipes: Thank you for showing up and bringing these meals into your homes. Cathy St Germans, Alli and Nick Christenson, Kyle McBurnie, Shae and Casey Gospel, Kim and Mark Healey, Eli Olson, Rayne Gourley, Jess Rohr, Sonnaly and Justin Lee, Jock Southerland, Lianne and Andy Tamasese, Kiley Umeda and Lance Moe, Rebecca Villegas, Perrin James, Katye Killebrew, Ciara Lacy, Liz and Kristian House, Lynne Johnson, Laura Moritz, Angie Murphy, Katie Pere, Melissa and Joe Casale, Daniela Menkewicz, Brandee Taylor, Agatha Beins, Kevin Nellen, Todd Erskine, Lucy Green, Sam Potter, Holly Ford, Allie and Ryan Torres, Jen Alarcon, and Aunty Megz. If I am forgetting anyone, I love you and thank you!

To Liza Gill of the Pālehua Conservation Initiative, for the care you give to that beautiful mountain and for letting us stay there and write.

Buddy, I know it can't be easy to share your mama with so many people all the time. But I hope you know that you make my world go round. Thank you for being my son. I love you.

And from Jenny—thank you to Simon, Evie, and Julian. Love you!

And thank you to every plant and animal who nourished us through the recipe-making process of this book.

patagonia®

Index

TEN SPEED PRESS
An imprint of the Crown Publishing Group
A division of Penguin Random House LLC
1745 Broadway
New York, NY 10019
tenspeed.com
penguinrandomhouse.com

Typefaces: Font Bureau's Benton Sans and The Designers Foundry's Romek Sharp.

Library of Congress Cataloging-in-Publication Data is on file with the publisher.
LCCN: 2025031086

Hardcover ISBN 978-0-593-83714-6
Ebook ISBN 978-0-593-83715-3

Editor: Kelly Snowden | Production editor: Sohayla Farman
Assistant editor: Gabby Ureña Matos
Designer: Emma Campion
Production designers: Mari Gill and Faith Hague
Production and prepress color manager: Jane Chinn
Photo assistants: Madeleine Rosenthal and Carly Zech
Copy editor: Mi Ae Lipe | Proofreaders: Rachel Holzman, Miriam Garron, Tess Rossi, and Christina Caruccio
Indexer: Eldes Tran
Publicist: Kristin Casemore | Marketer: Brianne Sperber

Manufactured in Malaysia

10 9 8 7 6 5 4 3 2 1

First Edition

Cover photographs by Nicole Gormley

The authorized representative in the EU for product safety and compliance is Penguin Random House Ireland, Morrison Chambers, 32 Nassau Street, Dublin D02 YH68, Ireland, https://eu-contact.penguin.ie.